**Becky Goldsmith and
Linda Jenkins**

the BEST-EVER
Appliqué Sampler
from Piece O' Cake Designs

5 Projects, 9 Blocks
to Mix, Match & Combine

C&T PUBLISHING

Text and Artwork copyright © 2013 by Becky Goldsmith and Linda Jenkins

Photography and Artwork copyright © 2013 by C&T Publishing, Inc.

Publisher: Amy Marson

Creative Director: Gailen Runge

Art Director: Kristy Zacharias

Editor: Lynn Koolish

Technical Editor: Alison M. Schmidt

Cover/Book Designer: April Mostek

Production Coordinator: Jessica Jenkins

Production Editor: Joanna Burgarino

Illustrator: Becky Goldsmith

Photography by Christina Carty-Francis and Diane Pedersen of C&T Publishing, Inc., unless otherwise noted

Published by C&T Publishing, Inc., P.O. Box 1456, Lafayette, CA 94549

Library of Congress Cataloging-in-Publication Data

Goldsmith, Becky, 1956-

  The best-ever appliqué sampler from Piece O' Cake designs : 5 projects, 9 blocks to mix, match & combine / Becky Goldsmith and Linda Jenkins.

    pages cm

  ISBN 978-1-60705-471-9 (soft cover)

1. Appliqué--Patterns. 2. Patchwork--Patterns. 3. Quilting. I. Jenkins, Linda, 1943- II. Piece O'Cake Designs. III. Title.

  TT779.G62944 2013

  746.44'5--dc23

                    2012037626

Printed in China

10 9 8 7 6 5 4 3 2 1

Acknowledgments

We wouldn't be where we are without *you*. Thank you for using our patterns and reading our books. We love to see the way you incorporate our designs into the wonderful quilts you make. You keep us going.

Many people at C&T Publishing have been very good to us. First, Todd Hensley, CEO, welcomed us with open arms. Amy Marson, publisher, is always there to support us. Lynn Koolish, our editor, is the person we work with the most, and she has helped to make each and every book better. We appreciate the help that all of them have given to us.

It would be nice to be perfect, but we aren't, so we are very grateful to Alison Schmidt, technical editor, who makes sure we get the details right, and to Jessica Jenkins, the production coordinator, who kept everything in this complicated book on track. Diane Pederson has an eye for photography that we greatly appreciate. April Mostek, this book's designer, has given *The Best-Ever Appliqué Sampler* its distinctive appearance. We thank you all for your excellent efforts.

Dedications

From Becky

I believe that you really can learn something new every day. To do that you must let yourself be open to new ideas.

When presented with a new way to do something, it is easy to let your first thought be, "No, I do it *this* way." I have been guilty of that myself. However, in the last few years I have made a concerted effort to be more open to new ideas. As a consequence, I have learned some new things (not all of them appliqué related).

I dedicate this book to the spirit of open-mindedness and sharing that is such an important part of every quilter's life.

From Linda

My niece Magen is a marine biologist. She has a love for new adventures, like swimming with the whales, dolphins, and sharks (small, well-fed sharks). Magen loves the outdoors, hiking, rock climbing, being with the crew on a tall ship, and more. For the last few years Magen has worked on Catalina Island, teaching children about marine life.

I asked her once where this love of the outdoors came from. She looked at me and said, "Aunt Linda, you have been taking me hiking since I was five."

I dedicate this book to everyone who loves a new adventure. Not all adventures have to be outside. I hope you will have many wonderful hours with the adventure of needle-turn appliqué in this book.

Contents

Introduction

Time flies! It has been six years since we last updated
The New Appliqué Sampler, and the time has come to make changes
and add more information. Although our techniques have not
changed significantly over the years, we have more techniques and
tips to share with you. You can even watch demonstrations of
some of the techniques on our website, www.pieceocake.com.
Whether you are new to appliqué or are very familiar with
our techniques, this book is for you. **Happy stitching**!

Getting Started

Basic Supplies

FABRIC: All of the fabrics used in these quilts are 100% cotton. We recommend that you always prewash your cotton fabric.

DESIGN WALL: There are a variety of design wall options. No matter which you choose, this is a tool you need. Our design walls are made from 1"-thick insulation foam that is available in 4´ × 8´ sheets. Use as many sheets as necessary to cover your space. They are easy to cut. We attached them to our walls with sheetrock screws. Becky's design wall is covered with white flannel; Linda's, with batting.

APPLIQUÉ THREAD: Use cotton thread with cotton fabric. There are many brands to choose from. Try different brands until you find the one that works best for you. For hand appliqué, we recommend Superior MasterPiece 50-weight 2-ply cotton (available only on bobbins), Aurifil 50-weight cotton, and DMC 50-weight machine embroidery thread.

MACHINE-QUILTING THREAD: For our machine quilting, we usually use the threads listed above. We want the appliqué to be enhanced by the quilting, not to be overshadowed by it. We like the matte finish of cotton thread. We quilt our quilts heavily, so the lighter-weight threads work well. However, if you plan to quilt far apart or want more visible quilting stitches, you should use a heavier thread.

HAND-QUILTING THREAD: We like Gütermann's cotton hand-quilting thread. Perle cotton in size 16 or 12 is nice when you want bigger, more visible stitches.

PINS: Use ½" sequin pins to pin the appliqué pieces in place. Use larger flower-head quilting pins to hold the positioning overlay in place.

NEEDLES: For hand appliqué, Linda uses a size 11 Hemming & Son milliners (or straw) needle. Becky uses a Clover size 12 Black Gold sharp. There are many good needles available on the market. Find the one that fits *your* hand.

SCISSORS: Use embroidery-size scissors for both paper and fabric. Small, sharp scissors are better for precise cutting.

ROTARY CUTTER, MAT, AND ACRYLIC RULER: When trimming blocks to size and cutting borders, rotary-cutting tools will give you the best results.

PENCILS: To draw around templates onto fabric, we use a General's Charcoal white pencil or a mechanical chalk pencil that holds a 9mm refill. Both Sewline and Bohin make these pencils. We use either the white or the gray chalk, depending on the color and value of the fabric.

PERMANENT MARKERS: To make the positioning overlay, a black Sharpie Ultra Fine Point Permanent Marker works well on clear or frosted vinyl. The Faber-Castell Quilter's Pen Set from C&T Publishing works well also, and these pens are erasable when you use them on vinyl.

CLEAR OR FROSTED VINYL: Use a clear or frosted flexible, medium-weight upholstery vinyl or Quilter's Vinyl to make the positioning overlay. Frosted vinyl is transparent when placed on fabric. If the vinyl you buy comes with tissue paper, keep the tissue paper for storage. If your quilt shop does not have vinyl, look for it online or in stores that carry upholstery fabric.

CLEAR, SINGLE-SIDED, HEAVYWEIGHT SELF-LAMINATING SHEETS: We use these sheets to make templates. You can find these sheets at www.pieceocake.com, at most office supply stores, at some warehouse markets, or online. Buy the single-sided sheets, not the pouches. If you can't find laminating sheets, use clear Con-Tact paper—it will work in a pinch.

Appliqué supplies

SANDPAPER BOARD: When tracing around templates onto fabric, place the fabric on the sandpaper side of the board. Then place the template on the fabric. You'll love the way the sandpaper holds the fabric in place when you trace. We recommend the Essential Sandboard from Piece O' Cake Designs.

WOODEN TOOTHPICK: Use a round wooden toothpick to help turn under the turn-under allowance at points and curves. Wood has a texture that grabs and holds the fabric.

FUSIBLE WEB: If you prefer to fuse and machine stitch the appliqué, use a paper-backed fusible web and follow the manufacturer's instructions. It's a good idea to test the fusible web on the fabric you will be using.

EQ PRINTABLES: These are sheets of fabric that are already prepared for printing on an inkjet printer and are perfect for computer-generated documentation labels. This fabric comes in a variety of sizes in addition to the standard 8½" × 11" sheet.

NONSTICK PRESSING SHEET: If you are doing fusible appliqué, a nonstick pressing sheet will protect the iron and ironing board.

FULL-SPECTRUM WORK LIGHT: These lamps give off a bright, natural light. A floor lamp is particularly nice, because you can position it over your shoulder. Appliqué is much easier when you can see what you are doing.

BATTING: We prefer to use cotton batting. Several good batts are on the market. It is a good idea to do some research to find the batt that suits you best. Currently we are using Mountain Mist Blue Ribbon or Cream Rose, Quilter's Dream, and Tuscany by Hobbs.

QUILTING GLOVES: These gloves make it easier to hold on to the quilt during machine quilting. We use the Machingers brand.

SEWING MACHINE: Successful machine piecing and quilting requires the best sewing machine and table that you can afford. For piecing, we use Bernina machines. For machine quilting, we each use the Sweet Sixteen by Handi Quilter.

Fabric Preparation

Prewash your fabric before using it. Why?

- Prewash to remove excess dye and other chemicals in the cloth.

- Most cotton fabrics will shrink when washed and dried. Different fabrics shrink at different rates; it is better if the fabric shrinks *before* you sew it into the quilt.

- The turn-under allowance on your appliqué pieces will fray less if you wash and dry your fabric. Frayed edges can be hard to work with in hand appliqué.

- Fabric off the bolt has a finish that makes it a little slick. Washing removes this finish. In both piecing and appliqué, we find it much easier to sew together fabrics that are not sliding against each other.

- Prewashed fabric feels and smells better in your hand.

About Our Fabric Requirements

Cotton fabric is usually 40"–42" wide off the bolt. To be safe, we calculate all our fabric requirements based on a 40" width.

Use the fabric requirements for each quilt as a guide, but remember that the yardage amounts can vary depending on how you cut the fabric. Our measurements allow for some fabric shrinkage and minor errors in cutting.

Seam Allowances

All machine piecing is designed for ¼" seam allowances.

Borders

This book's cutting instructions are mathematically correct. However, variations in the finished size of the quilt top can result from slight differences in seam allowances. You should *always* measure your quilt before adding borders. When measuring, be sure to measure through the middle of the quilt top, not at the outer edges, which can stretch. Adjust the size of your borders if necessary.

Hand Appliqué or Fusible Web?

What's the Difference between Hand, Fusible, and Machine Appliqué?

All appliqué begins with a drawing. You can use almost any appliqué method with almost any appliqué pattern. It is important to choose the method that makes you happy and produces the look you want in your quilt.

Hand appliqué is the most traditional form of appliqué. The edges of the appliqué pieces are sewn by hand, which produces a softer look and feel. The turn-under allowance adds a bit of height at the edge of the appliqué. The added height from the turn-under allowance adds a feeling of depth that is not found in fused appliqué.

Why do we prefer *hand* appliqué? The true answer is that we enjoy handwork. As a matter of fact, we more than enjoy it—we love it! With stitching in hand, we are calmer, happier, and more able to deal with the stresses around us. It's better than therapy!

Hand appliqué is portable. You can stitch almost anywhere—waiting at the doctor's office, during breaks at work, riding (not driving!) in the car, or watching TV. It is surprising how much stitching you can do in the odd moments of your day.

In *fusible appliqué*, fabrics are *glued* together, most often with an iron-on fusible web. Fusible appliqué is faster than hand appliqué. It is also very flat, with clearly defined edges. Fused quilts can be stiff. Sometimes only the outer edges of the appliqué pieces are fused, in which case the center of the appliqué is softer.

There is some debate about the effect that fusible webs and fabric glues have on fabric. Only time will tell the long-term effect of these products.

Machine appliqué very often involves fusing the appliqué pieces to the background fabric and then finishing the edges on the sewing machine. If you leave the edges raw, they can sometimes fray. Many quilters machine stitch around those raw edges. Others use a turn-under allowance (sometimes secured with glue) and then finish the edge of the appliqué with machine stitching.

Machine appliqué, done well, takes time and skill.

Hand appliqué is the primary focus of this book. Where appropriate, we have included instructions for fusible web. If you choose to use fusible web in your quilt, please test the fabrics you plan to use and follow the manufacturer's instructions carefully.

Color, Contrast, and Value

The Importance of Color

It's easy to see why so many quilters think that color is *the* most important part of a quilt. Color makes you look. It can evoke emotions. However, color by itself is not the most important part of your quilt.

Every color has a *value*. It will be light, medium, dark, or somewhere in between. *Contrast* is the difference between two or more values. *The contrast between different values makes a design visible.* Where fabrics high in contrast meet, they are very visible. Fabrics low in contrast placed next to each other blend together.

Look at the fabrics below. Yes, they are different shades of blue, and yes, they are different prints—but they are all medium value.

Even though fabrics are different, the similarity in color and value makes it hard to see differences between them.

Because these fabrics are so similar in both color and value, it is difficult to tell them apart from a distance. Using only these fabrics in a quilt is a waste of your time if you want people to actually see the pattern.

Adding more values to the original stack of fabric gives you a variety of lights, mediums, and darks with which to work. Using a range of values will help you to see the differences between fabrics.

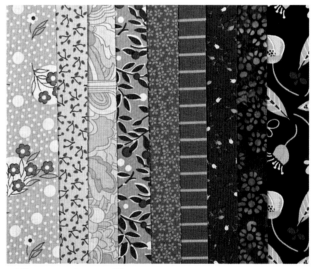

Adding more values provides more contrast.

Placing fabrics high in contrast next to each other in your quilt is one sure way of making that part of the design stand out. If you want to subdue an area, use fabrics that are lower in contrast. Many quilts have areas of both high and low contrast.

*Be aware that just because two fabrics are different **colors** does not mean that the fabrics are different **values**.* The blue and green to the right are different colors, but they look nearly the same. If you use them next to each other in a quilt, you may not be able to distinguish blue pieces from green pieces. That can ruin a design.

Remember also that value is relative. A light yellow may be visible against a dark yellow, but the darkest yellow will still look very light against black.

Fabrics that are different colors but similar values blend together and make a design less visible.

Designs on Fabric

Fabric comes in solid colors—and everything else.

Solid colors are just that, solid color. It's easy to think of solids as boring, but that's not true. Quilts from Amish to modern that are made with only solid fabrics are wonderfully graphic. Many of today's art quilters use solids much as they would use paint to create amazing quilts.

Quiet versus loud

The "everything else" category of fabric is pretty crowded. Solids, tone-on-tones, and low-contrast prints tend to be quiet. Other fabrics are loud and busy. Busy fabrics tend to be prints that are composed of high-contrast colors or values. Big, busy prints are fun and exciting.

Both quiet and loud fabrics can have a place in appliqué. That said, remember that your appliqué will be easier to see on a quieter background. Small appliqué pieces can get lost on a busy background.

Scale refers to the size of the design on the fabric. Large-scale designs look different from small-scale designs. A printed fabric can have any design imaginable on it: tiny little dots, huge flowers, stripes. The list is endless!

Small-, medium-, and large-scale prints

Fabric stacks from *Fanciful Flowers* (page 90)

Choosing Fabric for a Quilt

Before we begin a quilt, the first thing we decide is what colors we want to work with—what is making us happy right then. We make a stack of fabrics for each new quilt. In that stack are fabric choices for the backgrounds and for the appliqué. We don't worry about where we will use each fabric; that comes later. For now we focus on fabric that we think might belong in the quilt we are about to make. We begin the stack with fabric from our stashes, adding new fabric from the quilt store as necessary.

When starting your quilt, *you have to decide* what *you* want to use. If you tend to struggle with your color choices, you may be overthinking it. In some ways this is like deciding what clothes you want to put on in the morning. See, you already have practice making color choices!

You can begin by choosing at least one color that you really want to work with and then adding to it. We tend to choose the background color first. Monochromatic (one-color) color schemes are simpler to work with than very colorful, scrappy color schemes. Quilts made from two values (light and dark) are simpler than more complex mixes of values. You can look at the quilts in this book or in other books for inspiration. In fact, if you keep your eyes open, you will find inspiration all around you.

After you have decided on colors and selected fabric, separate the background fabric from the appliqué fabric. If you have several background fabrics, stack them from darkest to lightest. This is not as hard as it sounds. Look at the background fabric in front of you and choose the darkest piece. Start the stack with this piece. Continue choosing the darkest fabric and placing it on the stack. You may or may not be able to use all of these fabrics.

Next, sort the appliqué fabrics by color. You might have a green stack, a red stack, a blue stack, and so on. Sort each color from dark to light as described above. Some fabrics could go in more than one stack: Does this orange belong in the red group? You can merge color stacks, blending from one color into another.

Are you wondering why you are sorting and stacking your fabric? What we have found is that it's easier to work from an organized group of fabric than it is to work from a disorganized pile. The more you arrange and rearrange the fabric in your stack, the more color combinations you will discover.

Place your stacks next to each other. Does the background work with the appliqué fabric? Do you have the necessary light, medium, and dark values to make your quilt? Are the colors working together? Any fabric that doesn't look good in the stack is not likely to look any better cut up and sewn into your quilt. This is the time to remove any fabric that doesn't work. If a fabric isn't working, force yourself to put it away.

Clear Colors versus Gray Colors

When you look into the distance, colors get grayer. The colors in objects close to you are sharp and clear, but with each step away, more dust and dirt and water is in the air, which reduces the clarity of the colors.

When you use both clear and gray colors together in a quilt, the clear colors appear to come forward. Gray or muddy colors recede. In an appliqué quilt, it is best to put the grayer colors in the background.

If you have a fabric that looks bad in the stack, it may be that it is either too clear or too gray to work well with the rest. Not every fabric works in every quilt.

Many colors live in the middle—they look gray in one stack of fabrics and clear in another. Adding some of these fabrics to your stack can add visual depth to your quilt.

Gray colors and clear colors

If you have trouble knowing if the fabrics in your stack look good together, stand back and squint at them. Better yet, take a digital picture of them. Sometimes you see more in a photo than you do when you're looking at the real thing. If you are happy with your choices, it's time to move on. You can always add or remove fabric as you work.

Color Tip

Sometimes you see a quilt in a book or magazine or quilt show and just *love* it! You want to make one just like it. You can learn a lot about how to use color, contrast, and value by using the original quilt as a guide. But eventually you'll be ready to use color your own way. When that day comes, make a black-and-white copy of the color photo you fell in love with. This grayscale "map" of the quilt will help you place the light, medium, and dark values. Working with the black-and-white copy will also make it easier for you to see the quilt in the colors *you* want to use.

Audition Time

We cut and place every fabric in position on the design wall before we take a stitch. Always. By doing this, we *know* that the quilt is going to be wonderful before we put all those stitches into it.

First, put the backgrounds on the design wall. If you are going to piece your background, put all the different pieces on the wall. Sew the background blocks together only when you are sure they are balanced and work well together.

Next, starting with the first block, trace and cut out the appliqué pieces. Begin with whatever piece seems like the most obvious choice to you. Add the 3/16" turn-under allowance and cut carefully. Use your overlay and place each piece on the wall as you go. (Refer to the information on preparing the appliqué and making and using the overlay, pages 15–24.)

On the design wall, each fabric is auditioning for its role in the quilt. Some fabrics will not make the cut. Others will be perfect. You really don't know until you see them in place on the wall. *You can't fake the audition.* Sticking some fat quarters on the wall and hoping for the best doesn't work. Trust us; we know.

You will find as you read further that some appliqué shapes are easier to sew if you cut them out with excess fabric around them (see Cutaway Appliqué on page 52). This is especially true with small, narrow, or reverse appliqué shapes. This means you won't use every appliqué piece you have on the wall. Some pieces will be sacrificed because you will need to recut them for sewing. But your quilts will be so much better if you see every piece cut to shape (with its turn-under allowance) before you start stitching.

We work through one block at a time, until all the appliqué pieces are on the wall, even the borders. We place sashing strips, inner borders, everything that is part of that quilt, on the wall.

Are you done? Take a giant step back and really look at your work. Begin stitching the appliqué only when you are happy with all of your fabric choices.

Taking the Pieces Off the Wall

After all the pieces are cut out and auditioned—and you are happy—you need to take the pieces off the wall.

We have designed a felt-lined storage folio to carry appliqué pieces. It is a very compact and portable way to keep your appliqué pieces flat and in order. You can also make your own simple appliqué carrier. Fold a sheet of paper in half. Cut a piece of flannel or felt 5½" × 8½". Open the folded paper and place the flannel or felt inside it.

Take your appliqué pieces off the wall starting with the highest number—the piece you will sew last. Place this piece right side up at the bottom of the felt page. Continue taking the pieces off the wall in reverse order, overlapping as necessary to create a sloped stack of appliqué pieces that ends with the #1 piece on top. Fold the paper book closed with the appliqué pieces inside. The flannel or felt keeps the fabric from shifting, and the paper adds stability. Place the folio in our Quilter's Appliqué Caddy or in a similar project bag.

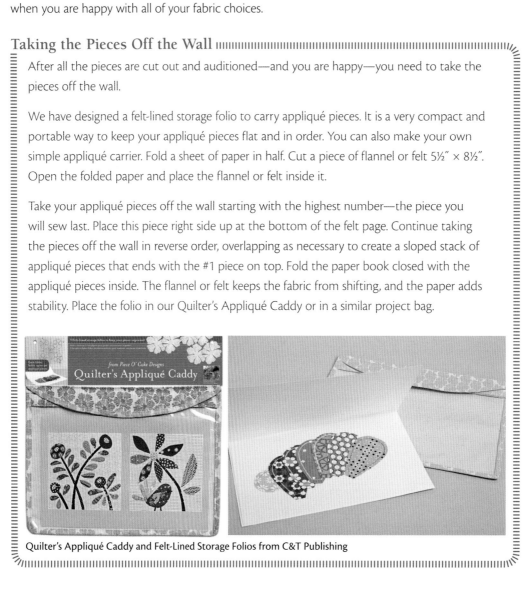

Quilter's Appliqué Caddy and Felt-Lined Storage Folios from C&T Publishing

General Instructions

Project Instructions

Read through all the instructions before beginning a project. Then you can refer back to specific techniques as needed.

Stitching Order

Our appliqué patterns are numbered to indicate the stitching sequence. Begin with appliqué piece #1, and work your way through the block.

Look at the drawing of the Wreath block below. Notice that there are numbered pieces in only one quadrant of the block. That tells you that the other four quadrants are the same. You only need to make one template for each shape.

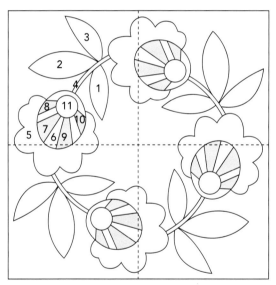

All four quadrants of this block are the same.

A Note about the Wreath Block

If you look at the Wreath pattern (pullout page P3), you will see different numbers in parentheses. You can sew the flowers with either one large petal or five smaller petals. The flower centers are sewn using off-the-block construction (page 61).

When you appliqué a block like this, you might be tempted to stitch one quadrant at a time. However, doing so can cause your background to draw up unevenly, making it harder to position additional appliqué pieces. We recommend that you sew all of the #1 pieces, then all of the #2 pieces, and so on. This will help your block retain its shape.

Preparing the Backgrounds for Appliqué

The outer edges of the block can stretch and fray as you handle it while stitching. The appliqué can shift during stitching and your stitches can cause the block to shrink slightly. For these reasons, when you cut out the backgrounds, it is best to add 1" to all sides. We have included this amount in the cutting instructions for each quilt. You will trim the blocks to size after the appliqué is complete.

1. Cut backgrounds as directed in the pattern. For blocks with pieced backgrounds, cut and sew the backgrounds together as directed.

2. Press each background block in half vertically and horizontally. This establishes a center grid in the background that will line up with the center grid on the positioning overlay. If your block is pieced with 4 identical squares, you can use the seamlines instead of pressing.

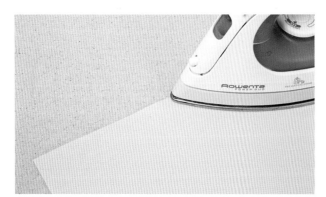

Press background in half in one direction.

Press background in the other direction.

3. With a pencil or permanent marker, draw a mark ¼" long on each end of the pressed grid lines. Do not make the lines too long or they will show on the block. These little lines will make it easier to position the overlay correctly as you work. These lines also make it easier to keep your appliqué centered when you trim the block to size.

Mark the ends of the pressed lines.

4. With a pencil or permanent marker, draw a little X in the upper right corner of the block background. This X will be in the same corner as the X that you will draw on the overlay. These will be registration marks that allow you to always line up your block and overlay correctly.

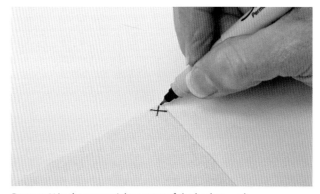

Draw an X in the upper right corner of the background.

Even Better!

When your blocks are on your design wall, you can see how they fit together in the quilt. But after you take them off the wall, it can be hard to remember which block goes where. If each block is identical, this isn't a problem. But if the blocks are not identical, you need an easy way to get them back into place in the quilt.

This is what we do: When the blocks are on the design wall in their final position, we number the background

in the upper right corner. This number replaces the X as a registration mark. You can then see at a glance how the block is oriented and its position in the quilt. You can put more information at the edge of your background block if you like: the name of the pattern, the date, or whatever is important to you.

Making the Appliqué Templates

Each appliqué shape requires a template, and we have a unique way to make templates that is both easy and accurate.

You will notice how easy it is to cut out these templates. That's the main reason we like this method. A mechanical copy of the pattern is also more accurate than hand tracing onto template plastic. As you use the templates, you will see that they are sturdy and hold up to repeated use.

1. Photocopy each block. Make as many copies as you need to ensure that you have one whole paper shape for each piece that requires a template. Always compare the copies with the original to be sure they are the same size.

2. You are going to cover the template shapes with the self-adhesive laminate (page 7). There is no reason to laminate the parts of the copies that you aren't going to use. With that in mind, cut the appliqué shapes you need from the copies. Group shapes when you can. Leave a paper allowance around each shape or group. Where one shape overlaps another, cut the top shape from one copy and the bottom shape from another copy. You do not want a template with a hole in it.

More about Overlapping Shapes

Look at leaves 2 and 3 in the Vase of Flowers block (pullout page P2). Cut each leaf as a whole leaf. We like to connect the edges of the leaf with a pencil line before covering the copy with laminate.

3. Place a self-laminating sheet shiny side down on the table. Peel off the paper backing, leaving the sticky side of the sheet facing up.

4. If you are doing hand appliqué, place the templates right side down on the self-laminating sheet.

Use your templates right side up in needle-turn hand appliqué. You want the paper side of the template next to the fabric when you trace around your templates.

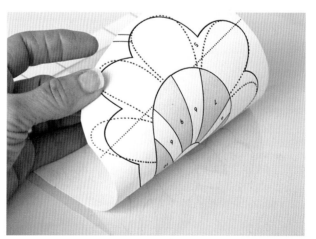

Face down for hand appliqué

When the paper touches the laminate, it will stick. You can't peel it off. It works best to *cup* the paper. Slowly and deliberately set the center of the paper on the sticky side of the laminate. Slowly lower the two sides of the paper onto the laminate.

If an edge of a shape didn't get covered, cut a bit of laminate and stick it where you need it, overlapping the edges of the plastic.

For fusible appliqué, place the *blank* side down onto the sticky side of the laminate.

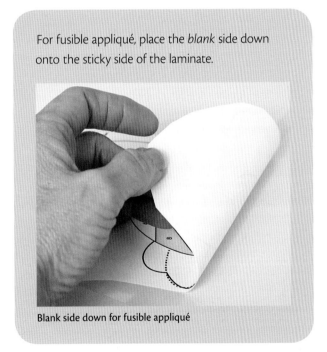

Blank side down for fusible appliqué

5. Cut out each shape. Try to split the drawn line; don't cut inside or outside this line. Keep the edges smooth and the points sharp.

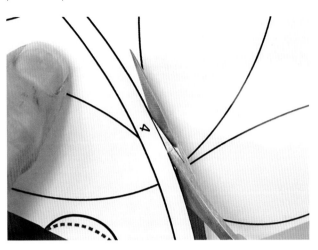

6. In reverse appliqué, as in the Going Home block (pullout page P2), cut shapes marked *reverse* out of the larger template.

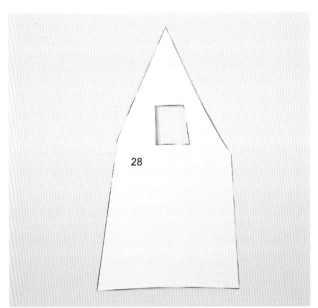

What if You Need a Big Template?

Some templates are bigger than a sheet of paper. In this case, copy the shape in sections. Match the paper shapes and tape them together with clear tape. Overlap pieces of laminate until the paper template shape is covered.

Using Templates for Hand Appliqué

For needle-turn hand appliqué, use the templates right side up on the right side of the fabric.

1. Place the appliqué fabric right side up on a sandpaper board (page 8).

2. Place the template right side up (shiny laminate side up) on the fabric so that as many edges as possible are on the diagonal grain of the fabric. A bias edge is easier to turn under than an edge on the straight of grain.

An exception to this is when a design in the fabric needs to go a certain way in that appliqué piece. In this case, place the template on the fabric to take advantage of the design in the fabric.

3. Trace around the template. The sandpaper board will hold the fabric in place while you trace. Be sure to draw the line right next to the edge of the template.

Make a line you can see! It won't matter if the line is wide, because it gets turned under. The chalk line is part of the turn-under allowance. If the line is too faint, you won't be able to see it when you are stitching.

4. Cut out each piece, adding a ³⁄₁₆″ turn-under allowance from the inside edge of the chalk line.

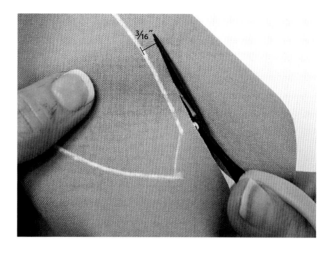

Turn-Under Allowance

A ³⁄₁₆″ turn-under allowance is smaller than ¼″ and bigger than ⅛″. A turn-under allowance that is too small will fray before you can sew it down. One that is too big will pleat as you turn it under. When the turn-under allowance is uneven, it is harder to turn under smoothly.

In areas where an appliqué piece is covered by another piece, cut the turn-under allowance bigger. We often leave as much as a ⅜″ allowance, knowing that we can trim excess fabric away later. It's really nice to have the extra fabric in case pieces shift during stitching.

Flipping Templates Over

Look at the side borders in *The Garden at My House* (page 84). The right border is a mirror image of the left border. You have the option of using the templates and overlay upside down. If this is what you choose, you must remember to turn the templates over when you are tracing the appliqué shapes for the right side border. That sounds obvious, but it's easy to forget when you are in the middle of tracing and cutting.

Because the slick plastic will be next to the fabric, templates will be a little harder to trace around. Hold the templates in place more carefully than you usually do. When you are stitching, remember to flip the overlay over. The numbers will be upside down but readable.

Using Templates for Fusible Appliqué

For fusible appliqué, use the templates with the drawn side down (shiny laminate side up) on the wrong side of the fabric.

1. Test the fusible web with the fabrics you plan to use.

2. Following the manufacturer's instructions on the fusible web, iron it to the *wrong* side of the appliqué fabric. Use a nonstick pressing cloth to protect the iron and ironing board. Do not peel off the paper backing.

3. Leave the fabric right side down. Place the template drawn side down (shiny laminate side up) and trace around it onto the paper backing of the fusible web.

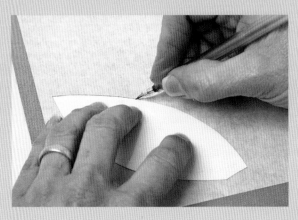

4. Cut out the appliqué pieces on the drawn line. Add a scant ³⁄₁₆″ allowance to any part of an appliqué piece that lies under another piece.

The Positioning Overlay

A positioning overlay is easy to make and use—and it makes your projects portable. Use it to position each appliqué piece accurately on the block. There is no need to draw the design on your background fabric. You don't need a lightbox to position your appliqué.

Finding the Right Vinyl

Make the positioning overlay from a piece of medium-weight, transparent upholstery vinyl. Look for vinyl that doesn't stretch easily and is relatively easy to pin through.

For years we used clear upholstery vinyl that comes on a roll with tissue paper. When this vinyl is folded or rolled, the tissue paper keeps the plastic from sticking together. After you have drawn on the vinyl, the tissue paper liner keeps the drawn lines from transferring from one part of the vinyl to another.

We recently discovered a frosted vinyl that does not come with, or require, tissue paper. This product is transparent when placed on top of fabric. It doesn't stretch, and it is easy to pin through. It is very easy to work with and we like it a lot. Frosted vinyl is available at www.pieceocake.com.

Quilter's Vinyl is clear vinyl that comes without tissue paper. This 16"-wide vinyl is also a good choice and is available in many quilt shops.

Making the Positioning Overlay

1. Cut a piece of the vinyl (and its tissue paper lining, if applicable) to the finished size of the block. Set the tissue paper aside until you are ready to fold or store the overlay.

2. Work directly from the patterns in this book or make a copy of them, whichever is easier for you.

3. Tape the pattern onto a table.

4. Tape the vinyl over the pattern. Use a ruler and a black Sharpie Ultra Fine Point Permanent Marker or the 0.4 mm

Faber-Castell Quilter's Pen (C&T Publishing) to draw the pattern's horizontal and vertical centerlines onto the vinyl.

5. Accurately trace all the lines from the pattern onto the vinyl. The numbers on the patterns indicate stitching sequence; include these numbers on the overlay. These numbers also tell you which side of the overlay is the right side.

6. Draw a small X in the upper right corner of the positioning overlay. This will be used to make sure the overlay is always used in the correct orientation (see Preparing the Backgrounds for Appliqué, page 15).

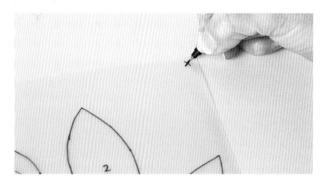

Finger-Pressing

Finger-pressing is a very important step! You'll be amazed at how much easier it is to turn under the allowance as you stitch.

Before you position and pin any appliqué piece to the block, finger-press it. Hold the appliqué piece right side up. Using your thumb and index finger, turn the allowance under to the back of the appliqué so that the chalk line is just barely turned under. If you can see the chalk line on top of the appliqué when you finger-press, it will be visible after it is sewn also.

Use your fingers to press a crease into the fabric along the inside of the chalk line. Do not wet your fingers, do not use starch, and do not scrape your fingernail along the crease. Just pinch it with your fingertips. Good-quality, 100% cotton will hold a finger-press very well.

Only the edges of an appliqué piece that will be turned under and stitched should be finger-pressed. You would not, for example, finger-press the line at the end of a leaf that indicates where it is covered by a stem. It *is* a good idea to finger-press beyond the end of a line, into the seam allowance at points.

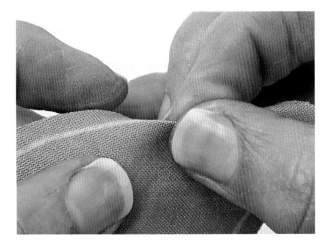

Using the Positioning Overlay for Hand Appliqué

1. Place the background right side up on your work surface. We like to work on top of our sandpaper board, because the sandpaper keeps the background from shifting as the appliqué is positioned.

2. Place the overlay right side up on top of the background fabric.

3. Line up the center grid in your background with the center grid of the overlay. Place the X on the overlay in the same corner as the X on the block (or the number, if you numbered your blocks).

4. Pin the overlay, if necessary, to keep it from shifting out of position. Flat flower-head pins work best for this. Place your pins near the area where you will be positioning appliqué pieces. Always remove the overlay from the block before you begin stitching.

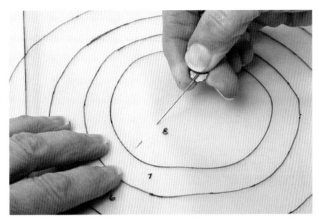

If necessary, pin the overlay in place.

5. Before placing appliqué pieces on the block, finger-press the turn-under allowances (page 22). *This is a very important step. Don't skip it!* As you finger-press, make sure that the drawn line is pressed to the back. You'll be amazed at how much easier this one step makes needle-turning the turn-under allowance.

6. Place the first piece under the overlay but on top of the background. It is easy to tell when the appliqué pieces are in position under the overlay—the drawn line on the appliqué fabric should "halo" the drawn line on your overlay. As you work, finger-press and position one piece at a time. Be sure to place the appliqué pieces on the block in numerical order.

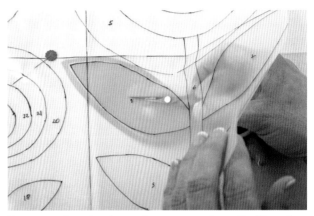

You can use the point of your scissors to move the appliqué into place.

7. Fold the positioning overlay back and pin the appliqué pieces in place using ½" sequin pins. You can pin against the sandpaper board; it does not dull the pins (see Pinning, pages 24–26).

8. If you are new to this technique, it's a good idea to use the positioning overlay to double-check the placement of the piece you just pinned. Remove the overlay before stitching.

9. The vinyl positioning overlay can be folded or rolled for storage. If your vinyl came with tissue paper, place the tissue paper over the drawn side before you fold it. The tissue paper keeps the lines from transferring from one part of the vinyl to another.

How Many Pieces Can You Pin to the Block at Once?

Imagine you have pinned three pieces to the block and that you are stitching them in sequence. By the time you get to the third piece, it needs to be in the same condition as it was when you first pinned it to the block. If it has stretched or frayed, it will be harder to stitch.

Consider the size, shape, and placement of the pieces, as well as the weave of the fabric, before pinning lots of pieces to your background at one time. We usually pin one or two pieces at a time.

Using the Positioning Overlay for Fusible Appliqué

1. Place the background right side up on the ironing board.

2. Place the overlay right side up on top of the background.

3. Line up the center grid in your background with the center grid of the overlay. Place the X on the overlay in the same corner as the X on the block (or the number, if you numbered your blocks).

4. Peel off the paper backing from each appliqué piece as you go. Be careful not to stretch or unravel the outer edges.

5. Place the appliqué pieces right side up under the overlay but on top of the background. Start with appliqué piece #1 and follow the appliqué order. Peel off the paper backing from each appliqué piece as you go. Be careful not to stretch or unravel the outer edges. It is easy to tell when the appliqué pieces are in position under the overlay.

You may be able to position several pieces at once.

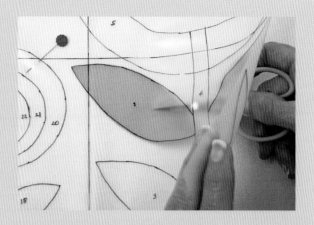

6. Carefully remove the overlay and iron the appliqué pieces in place. Do not touch the overlay vinyl with the iron because the vinyl will melt. Be sure to follow the manufacturer's instructions for your fusible web.

Tip

When using fusible web, it's a good idea to protect your iron by placing either an appliqué pressing sheet or Silicone Release Paper (C&T Publishing) between the appliqué and the iron.

7. Sewing the raw edges of the fused appliqué holds the edges of the appliqué securely in place. This is best done on the sewing machine using a blanket stitch or straight stitch.

Pinning

½″ Sequin Pins

Pin your appliqué pieces in place with ½″ sequin pins. These short pins take a little getting used to, but there are three big advantages to using them:

- Because they are short, you can use more pins to hold each piece in place. This prevents your appliqué from shifting out of position as you stitch.

- Your thread doesn't hang up on these short pins as much as it does on longer pins.

- When you are stitching, these short pins don't poke your holding hand the way long pins do.

1. *Do not pick up the block!* Pin with the fabric flat against your sandpaper board.

2. Pick up the pin and push it through both layers of fabric until you can feel the sandpaper below. Place the index finger of your other hand in front of the spot that you intend to pin. Shift your grip on the pin so that you can push it forward, scraping the sandpaper.

3. Lift up with the pin while pushing down on the fabric in front of the pin with your index finger. This makes a little hill through which you can push the tip of the pin.

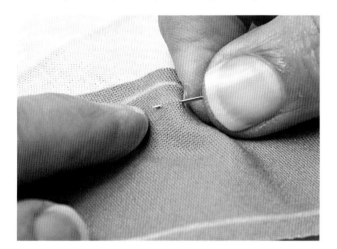

Pinning Sequence

The order in which you place your pins is important. We always pin the two points that are farthest apart first. This way the appliqué is less likely to shift during the pinning process.

1. Place your first pin in the spot that needs to stay put the most. In this example you would pin the base of the leaf first to keep it from moving out from under the stem. Next, pin the tip of the leaf.

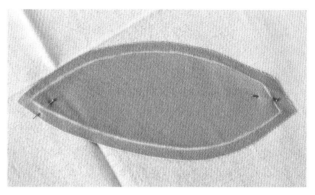

2. Fill in with as many pins as necessary. Don't overlap your pins—that stretches the fabric. You don't want your pins too far apart either—that can cause the edges of your appliqué to shift out of position as you stitch.

3. Make sure your pins are parallel to the outer edge. The pin does a better job of holding the fabric in place when it is parallel to the edge. Place your pins ¼" inside the chalk line. This leaves room for the turn-under allowance.

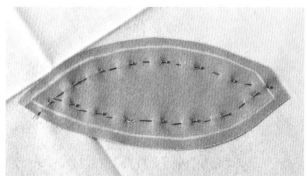

Pins should be parallel to the edge and ¼" inside the chalk line.

Pinning Outer Points

The pin at an outer point should hold the point in position as you stitch. Where you place your pin at an outer point depends on the direction in which you stitch.

It can be confusing to think about what direction you sew when you don't have your stitching in your hand. Refer to Outer Points (page 42) for information about stitching directions for outer points.

Do not pin outer points as shown to the right! This is *wrong*, because it allows the fabric at the end of the point to move around.

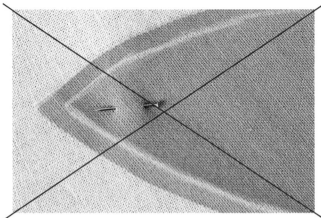

Do **NOT** pin outer points like this.

1. Outer points are sewn one side at a time. The trick is to identify the side of the outer point that you will sew first. Place your pin *parallel* to that side and ¼" away from it. Place the pin as far as you can toward the point so that the very tip of the point is held in place.

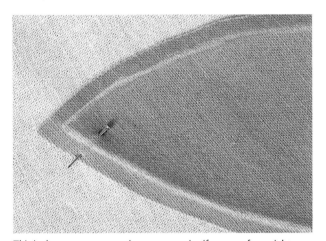

This is the correct way to pin an outer point if you sew from right to left, with the horizon.

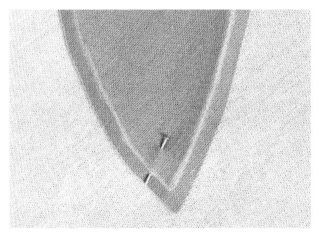

This is the correct way to pin an outer point if you are right-handed and sew from top to bottom on the right side of your appliqué. *Note to left-handers*: If you are left-handed, sewing from left to right with the horizon, your pin will look like this.

2. Notice that the pin falls over the line on the other side of the point. You will stitch the first side of the point (all the way to the point) and then remove this pin to sew the second side of the point. This pin won't be in your way. Don't worry—we'll tell you when to remove it.

Where Do You Begin Sewing?

Many appliqué pieces have an obvious place to begin sewing. Starting and stopping places are formed where one appliqué piece overlaps another. The leaf that we pinned earlier is a good example (page 25). The base of the leaf is covered by a stem. You will begin sewing where the stem meets the leaf. Sew around the leaf and stop on the other side where the leaf meets the stem again.

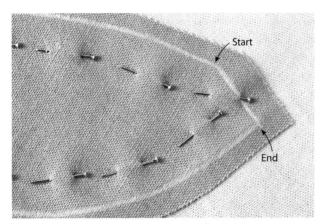

Begin and end sewing at the place where appliqué pieces meet.

On pieces that do not have an obvious starting spot (like a heart), begin at the *flattest* place. Never begin sewing at a

point that has to be turned and sewn—this is true for both outer and inner points. Do not start on sharp curves. If you are sewing a narrow curved strip like a stem, sew the concave side first if you can.

Free Spaces

You do not need to turn under and sew the parts of an appliqué piece that are covered by another appliqué piece. We like to think of these as free areas. When you look at an appliqué pattern, sometimes it can seem like there is an awful lot to stitch. But if you consider that only parts of each piece are actually stitched, it feels more manageable.

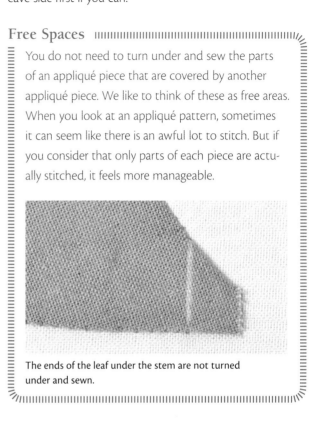

The ends of the leaf under the stem are not turned under and sewn.

Thread and Knots

We use 100% cotton thread with cotton fabric. We prefer to use the same fiber throughout the quilt—fabric, thread, and batting. Cotton thread has a matte finish that helps keep the stitches hidden. It is affordable, readily available in many colors, and easy to sew with. Cotton thread tolerates being ironed at high heat. Silk and polyester threads may be good choices for other projects, but we don't use them in our appliqué quilts.

Refer to Basic Supplies (page 7) to see the brands of thread we use. It is perfectly acceptable to mix different brands of thread to get the colors you need.

Choosing the Correct Thread Color

The appliqué thread will be invisible if it matches the appliqué fabric in both color and value. When we have to choose between a thread that is either a little lighter or darker, we choose the lighter thread.

Choosing a thread can be especially difficult when you are appliquéing a multicolor fabric. Unwind a few inches of all the threads that you think will work, and place the strands over the fabric. Which one is the least visible? That's the one to choose.

Threading the Needle

Sewing with thread that is too long will cause problems. You will find that working with thread that is 16"–20" long is good.

Why Does My Thread Get Twisted and Knotty?

Thread has a twist. The twist is what holds the cotton fibers together. When you overtwist your thread as you sew, it retains its shape but it twists together. If you untwist your thread as you sew, it gets kinks and knots and frays that make hand sewing less pleasant.

With every stitch you take, you may be turning the needle a little bit with your fingers. Right-handers tend to overtwist the thread as they sew. This is okay, although you may need to dangle the needle and let the thread relax every now and then.

If you are having a lot of trouble with knots and frays in your thread, pay attention to what you are doing with the needle as you sew. You may be adding a backward twist to the needle, which causes the thread to untwist.

Note to left-handers: Because you are sewing with your left hand, you may be more prone to untwisting the thread as you sew. If you are having problems, pay close attention to how you are handling the needle.

New News about Which End of the Thread to Knot

For years we truly believed that it made a difference which end of the thread got the knot. Well, we were wrong. If you are using a good-quality thread, it makes no difference which end of the thread gets the knot. Isn't it nice to have one less thing to worry about!

Traveling with Thread

To make our appliqué more portable, we carry our appliqué thread on bobbins. A bobbin holds a lot of thread. Superior's MasterPiece 50-weight 2-ply thread is available on prewound bobbins, or you can wind your own. If you wind your own, use clear, inexpensive plastic bobbins.

The Quilter's Knot

This is a great knot. It is big enough that it won't pull through the fabric but small enough that it's not bulky.

1. Hold the threaded needle in your hand. Hold the tail of the thread between your thumb and index finger, next to the needle. Leave a ⅜"–½" tail of thread.

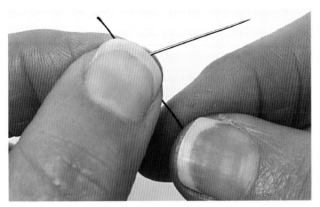

Right handers

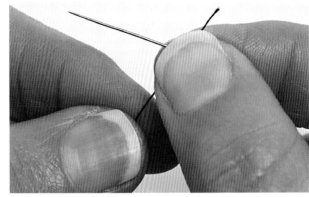

Left handers

2. While pinching the thread tail next to the needle, hold the thread with your other hand and wrap it 3 or 4 times. The finer the thread, the more wraps you will need to make a substantial knot.

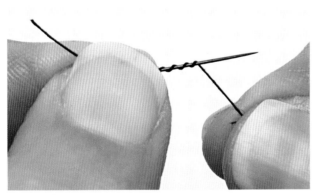

Right handers

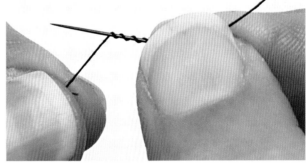

Left handers

3. Pull the wraps down the shaft of the needle until they are pinched with the thread tail between the thumb and index finger. Make sure you are holding the wraps; otherwise, your knot will fall apart.

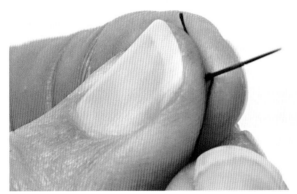

Right handers: Pinch down on the wraps so that they don't show.

Left handers: Pinch down on the wraps so that they don't show.

4. Gently pull the needle from your hand while still pinching the wraps and thread tail. Continue pulling until the knot is formed between your fingers.

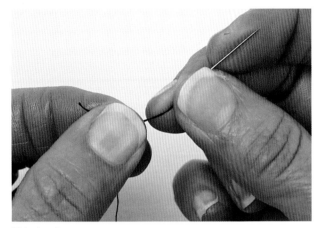

Right handers

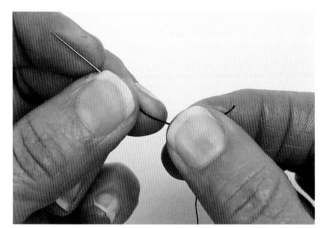

Left handers

5. If you want to trim the tail, don't cut it too close to the knot.

The Ending Knot

This quick little knot is very secure. We've heard it called a square knot and a surgeon's knot—we just call it the ending knot.

1. When you are ready to knot off your thread, send your needle to the back of your block. Take a small stitch in the background fabric, behind the appliqué, near the stitches. Pull the thread all the way through. This is your anchor stitch.

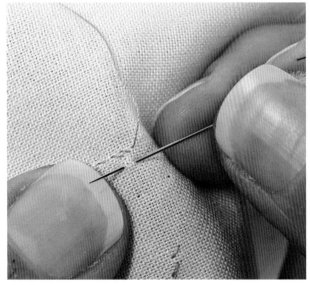

Right handers

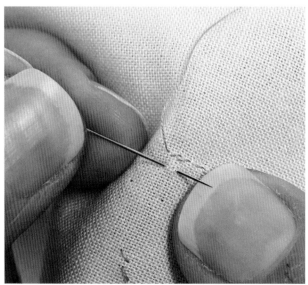

Left handers

2. Take another stitch through the anchor stitch and pull the thread slowly until a loop forms.

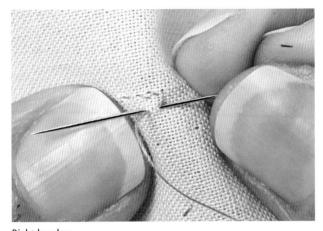

Right handers

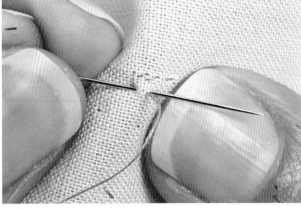

Left handers

3. Bring your needle and thread around the left side of the loop and then up through the loop from bottom to top. Pull the thread tight and the knot will form against your fabric.

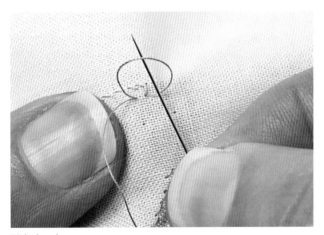

Right handers

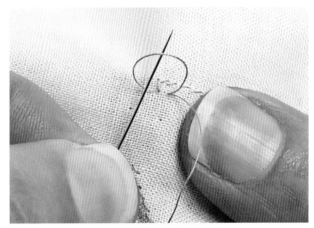

Left handers

4. Run the needle between the background and the appliqué to bury the tail of thread.

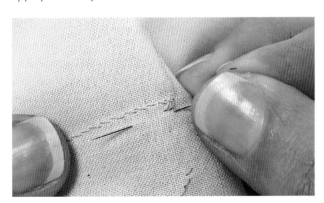

5. Cut the thread even with the back of the block.

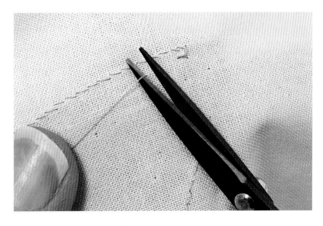

Pressing and Trimming the Blocks

1. After the appliqué is complete, press the blocks on the wrong side. If your ironing surface is hard, place the blocks on a towel so the appliqué will not get flattened. Be careful not to stretch the blocks as you press.

FYI ||||||||||||||||||||||||||||||||||||||||||||||||||||||||||

We very rarely trim away the fabric behind our appliqué. We believe leaving the background intact behind the appliqué adds stability and strength to the quilt as a whole. And should the quilt ever need to be repaired, it's easier if the background has not been cut.

We trim away fabric behind an appliqué only if a dark fabric is obviously shadowing through a lighter fabric or in the rare case when multiple pieced seams come together on top of each other.

2. Take your time when trimming your blocks to size. Be sure of your measurements *before* you cut. Remember to measure twice and cut once. All of the blocks in this book have a finished size of 14″ × 14″. Each block needs to be trimmed to 14½″ × 14½″.

3. Place a pressed block on the rotary cutting mat, right side up. The block should have a center mark on each of its 4 sides. Divide 14½″ by 2 to get 7¼″. Use the center marks and a ruler to measure 7¼″ out from the center of the block. If your ruler is too narrow, use more than one ruler.

Align center at 7¼″ mark.

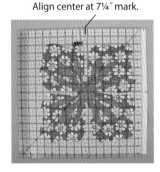

4. When you are sure you have measured correctly, trim the excess fabric along the right-hand side of the block.

Trimming Tips |||||||||||||||||||||||||||||||||||||||||||||||

- Always look carefully at your block before you trim. We add 1″ to each side of the finished size when we cut the background for each block and border. You should be trimming off about ¾″ from each edge of your blocks. If you are about to trim much more (or less) than that, check your measurements.

- Use the short lines that you drew over the ends of the pressed-in grid to help you center your cuts.

- Take your time. If it helps you visualize how much you need to trim away, compare your paper pattern with your block.

5. Rotate the block once, clockwise. Use the center mark at the top edge of the block and the newly cut straight side (now at the bottom of the block) to line up your ruler, and measure 7¼″ out from the center of the block. Cut away the excess fabric on this side of the block.

Align center at 7¼″ mark.

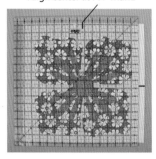
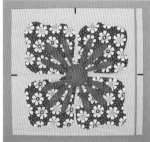

6. Measure 14½″ across the block from the 2 fresh cuts to finish trimming the block to size.

Appliqué Techniques

The Invisible Stitch

Sew your appliqué to your background with an invisible stitch. Doesn't that sound easy? It is, but it helps to have more specific information, and we are happy to share with you what we know.

Stitching Direction

People sew in a variety of directions, but the primary direction is from **right to left**, with the horizon. If you are left-handed, you probably sew from left to right, with the horizon.

It is less common for people to sew from **top to bottom**, with the open side of the appliqué on the right. We call this sewing vertically.

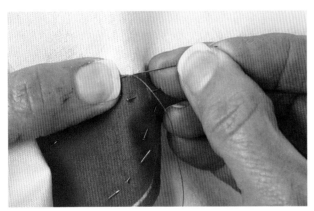

Right-handers sewing with the horizon

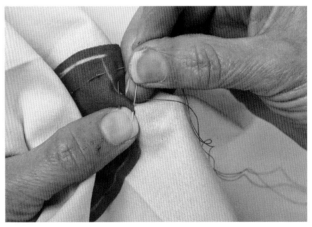

Sewing vertically

Both directions are correct. You are not wrong if you sew in a different direction from your stitch group buddy. We sew in different directions! Linda sews with the horizon; Becky sews vertically. That is how we discovered the very real differences between these two directions.

It is a bad idea to try to change the direction in which you sew unless you are having a lot of hand pain or are really unhappy with your stitch. Take time to look at the photographs (pages 35–41). Compare these photos with how you sew. Follow the instructions for the direction in which you sew.

No matter which direction you stitch, *always finger-press* your appliqué pieces *before* you pin them to your background (page 22). It really does make a difference!

Making a Good Stitch

After you know the mechanics of a good stitch, all your stitches will be invisible. Appliqué stitches are made one at a time. The needle goes into the background *next* to the edge of the appliqué fabric. The needle travels underneath the background fabric, following the edge of the appliqué fabric. The needle then comes back up through the background *and* the folded edge of the appliqué fabric in one fell swoop. It helps to go through this step by step.

Holding the Needle

Look at how we hold the needle. *It is most likely different from the way you are used to holding your needle.* Pick up your needle and hold it as shown. Imagine that the needle has become an extension of your index finger. The eye of the needle rests at the end of your index finger. Your thumb and middle finger hold the shaft of the needle, close to the end of your index finger. Your remaining two fingers should be curled comfortably nearby.

This is the way we hold our needle:

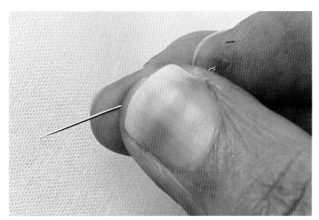

Holding the needle with the right hand

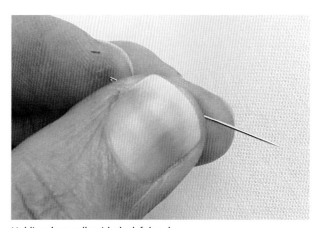

Holding the needle with the left hand

Yes, we can hear you! This new grip *is* different, and you *aren't* used to it. But before you throw your needle down, let us tell you the advantages of holding the needle this way. The best reason is that most people make a better stitch when they switch their grip on the needle. You are less likely to make a running stitch and more likely to make an invisible stitch. Most people find that their hands are much happier holding the needle this way, especially after hours of sewing.

It does take some practice to get used to this new grip. You'll find that you have to reposition the needle in your hand with each stitch. Trust us—it becomes automatic and very fast. As you look at the photos that follow, try to match your hand position to what you see.

Turning Under the Turn-Under Allowance

Most of the time, we use our needle to turn under the fabric edge; hence the name *needle-turn appliqué*. But there are times when a round wooden toothpick works better than the needle. There are even times when your fingertips are the best tool to use to turn the edge under.

When you are sewing long, nearly straight edges, you can turn under enough of the edge to make several stitches. In other places you will be able to turn under and control only *one stitch at a time*. Don't turn under more of the edge than you can control.

Remember that you turn your fabric under along the finger-pressed crease, which should graze the inside edge of the chalk line. Always finger-press your pieces before pinning them to the block (page 22).

Stitching Horizontally

This is the more common stitching direction.

Hold the block so that the edge you are going to stitch is roughly level with the horizon. The turn-under allowance is away from you, and the body of the appliqué piece is closer to you. You work over the top edge of the appliqué. If you are right-handed, hold the block in your left hand. If you are left-handed, hold the block in your right hand.

1. *Always* bring your thread up through the finger-pressed fold in the appliqué, just inside the chalk line. This ensures that the knot and tail of the thread will be hidden between the appliqué and the background. *Never* bring the thread up from the underside of your background fabric.

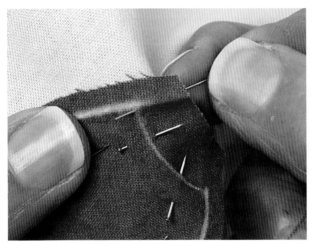

Right handers

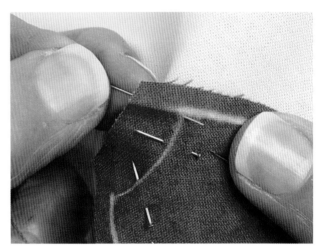

Left handers

2. Hold the needle perpendicular to the surface of your block. This helps you to make a more invisible stitch. Position the needle so that it is going into the background fabric next to the appliqué, next to the place where the thread came out of the appliqué fabric. You don't want the needle to go in either to the right or to the left of this spot.

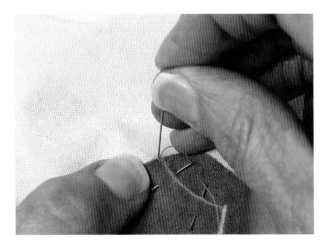

Right handers

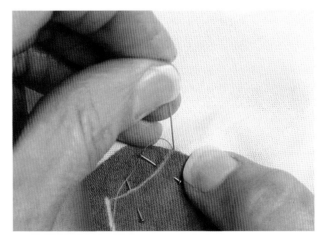

Left handers

3. The point of the needle goes through the background fabric to hit the tip of either the middle finger or the index finger of the holding hand, underneath the fabric. Your hand falls to the right (or left) as the needle rocks over the tip of your underneath finger. The needle advances under the background, following the edge of the appliqué.

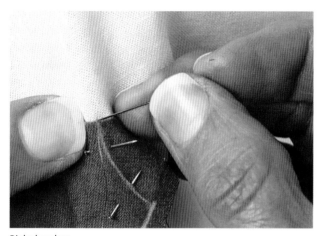

Right handers

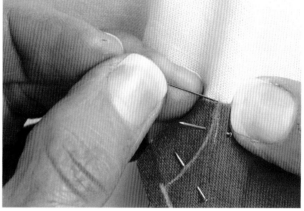

Left handers

4. Turn the needle to come up through the background fabric, just catching the folded edge of the appliqué.

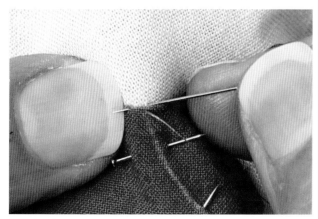

Right handers

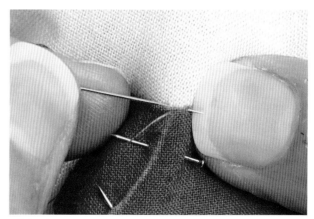

Left handers

5. The position of the hand holding the fabric is also important. Place the fabric in your hand so that the line you are sewing leads directly into the end of your thumb. Your left thumb should be sitting directly on top of the folded edge and be positioned so that when you stitch, the needle is pointed at the end of your thumb, not at the side of your thumb.

Why do you hold the fabric this way? Because your wrist will be in a more relaxed position and you will have less hand pain.

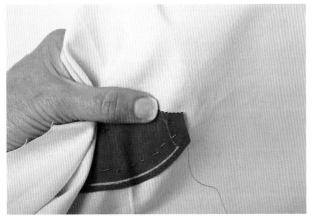

Right handers   Left handers

More about Thumb Placement

Your thumb holds in place the turn-under allowance that you have so carefully worked into position. As you rock off your bottom fingertip, the thumb helps make a hill to stitch through, much as it does in hand quilting. If you place your thumb correctly, as you bring your needle back up to the top, your stitch will go up through the fabric straight.

6. The end of your thumbnail (or your thumb tip if your nails are short) should be about ⅛" from the beginning of your stitch. Your needle will come up inside that, helping you to make a uniform stitch that is shorter than ⅛".

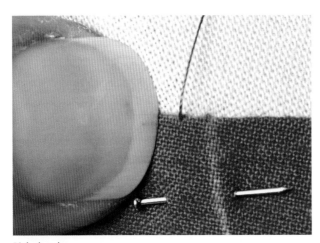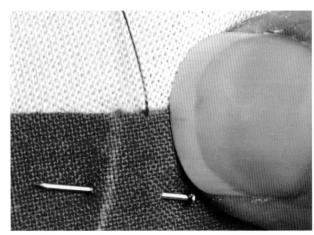

Right handers   Left handers

Stitching Vertically

This is the less common stitching direction.

Hold the block so that the edge you are going to stitch is nearly perpendicular to the horizon.

If you are right-handed, hold the block in your left hand. The turn-under allowance is on the right; the body of the appliqué piece is on the left. You work on the right side of the appliqué. Most of the time, your stitch is not absolutely vertical; it's more from the upper right to the lower left.

If you are left-handed, hold the block in your right hand. The turn-under allowance is on the left; the body of the appliqué piece is on the right. You work on the left side of the appliqué. Most of the time, your stitch is not absolutely vertical; it's more from the upper left to the lower right.

1. *Always* bring your thread up through the finger-pressed fold in the appliqué, just inside the chalk line. This ensures that the knot and tail of the thread will be hidden between the appliqué and the background. *Never* bring the thread up from the underside of your background fabric.

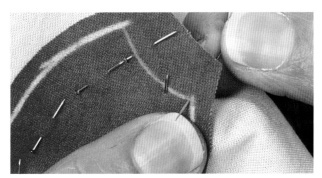
Right handers

Left handers

2. Hold the needle perpendicular to the surface of your block. This helps you to make a more invisible stitch. Position the needle so that it is going into the background fabric next to the appliqué, next to the place where the thread came out of the appliqué fabric. You don't want the needle to go in either to the top or to the bottom of this spot.

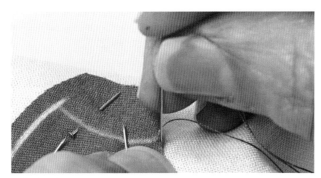
Right handers

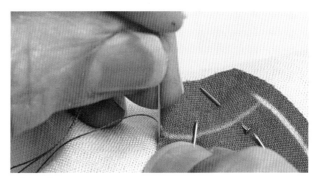
Left handers

Imagine a Diver

Sometimes it helps to imagine that the needle is a diver. The needle has come up through the background fabric and the folded edge of the appliqué. It then "dives" back into the background, next to the edge of the appliqué. Just as a diver enters the water perpendicularly, your needle should dive straight into the fabric.

3. The point of the needle goes through the background fabric to hit the tip of either the middle finger or the index finger of the holding hand, underneath the fabric. Your hand falls back as the needle rocks over the tip of your underneath finger. The needle advances under the background, toward you, following the edge of the appliqué.

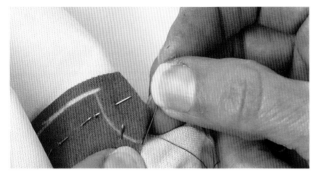

Right handers

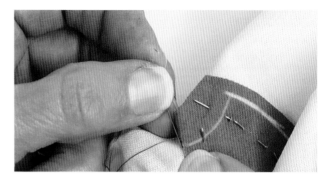

Left handers

4. Let your hand fall farther back so that the needle comes up through the background fabric, just catching the folded edge of the appliqué.

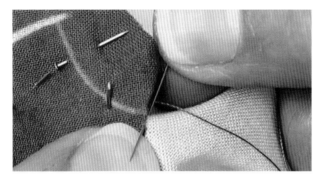

Right handers

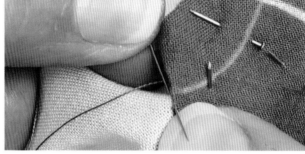

Left handers

5. The position of the hand holding the fabric is also important. Place the fabric in your hand so that the line you are sewing leads directly into the top corner of the thumbnail on your holding hand. Let the top of your thumb cover the folded edge of the appliqué. Be sure that your wrist is in a relaxed position. Avoid bending it into a cocked position.

Right handers

Left handers

More about Thumb Placement

Your thumb holds in place the turn-under allowance that you have so carefully worked into position. If you place your thumb correctly, as you bring your needle back up to the top, your stitch will go up through the fabric straight. As you rock off your bottom fingertip, the thumb helps make a hill to stitch through, much as it does in hand quilting.

6. Your thumbnail (or your thumb tip if your nails are short) should be about ⅛″ from the beginning of your stitch. Your needle will come up inside that, helping you to make a uniform stitch that is shorter than ⅛″.

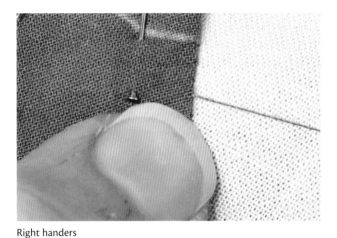

Right handers

Left handers

Stitch Length

The thumb of the holding hand determines the stitch length. If your thumb is too far from the needle, your stitch will be too long; too close, and your stitch will be too short. So, how long should your stitch be?

Imagine you are sitting down at your sewing machine to piece your quilt. How long would your stitches be? Eight stitches per inch is not enough—your seams would be loose and have gaps. You probably wouldn't set your stitch length to sixteen stitches per inch—that's a little bit too tight. You'd probably choose ten to fourteen stitches per inch on the machine. That's a good number of stitches for hand appliqué, too, except that your stitch length does shorten at inner and outer points and on inner and outer curves.

What Should the Back Look Like?

Your stitches should be angled because you are putting your needle into the fabric on one side of the edge of the appliqué and coming back up through it on the other side of the edge. Your stitches should not have any gaps or empty spaces between them.

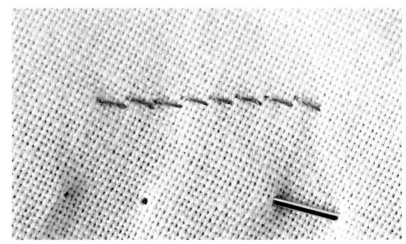

The stitches on the back should be angled, with no gaps between them.

If you have gaps between your stitches, either you are putting your needle into the fabric to the left (or right if you are left-handed) of the spot where the thread has come out of the fabric, or you are letting the needle travel back up through the layers at an angle. In either case, when you pull your stitches tight, the edge of the appliqué pleats up.

It is very important that the needle goes into the fabric right next to the edge of the appliqué and that the needle travels up through the layers straight— not at an angle.

Points

Points are everywhere in appliqué. You can't
avoid them, so why not master them!

You will get better at points as you stitch more of them.
Do not overwork any one point; it only gets worse. Instead,
stitch lots of points and you will see improvement.

Outer Points

A perfect point is one in which the turn-under allowance
is tucked away underneath the chalk lines on each side of
the point. If you turn under too much (or too little), the
point will be off.

Turning the first side of a point is easy. The second side is
the tricky part. You'll know the point is turned correctly
when the chalk line on the second side of the point is
turned under and is no longer visible on top. It is very
important that you are able to see the chalk lines on
your fabric. If you can't see the chalk line on your shape,
redraw it.

Most of the blocks in this book have outer points. All
outer points are worked in exactly the same way. To
practice, use any of the pointed leaves in this book.

Trimming Dog Ears

You may have heard quilters refer to the triangular tip of
fabric at the point of the turn-under allowance as the dog
ear. Some quilters cut off their dog ears; others don't. What
we have found is that it doesn't matter—unless you cut off
too much!

If you decide to cut off the dog ears, *be very careful to leave
a 3⁄16" seam allowance at the tip of the outer point.* If you
trim too much fabric, you will find that it is nearly impossible to turn the point without it fraying. Do not angle the
cut; keep it perpendicular to the point.

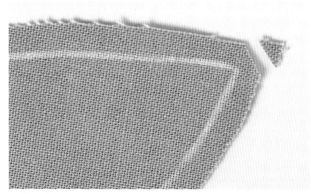

A clipped dog ear

More about Dog Ears

There are times when the end of a stem is not covered. Look at the stem in Going Home from *All Together Now* (pullout page P2) as an example. That uncovered stem has two outer points in close proximity to each other. It may help to trim the dog ears on these points to reduce the bulk. The following is a trick we learned from Nancy Pearson.

1. Extend the drawn seamlines at both points into the turn-under allowance.

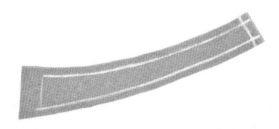

2. Cut off the dog ears from the end of one seamline to the end of the next seamline. Repeat for the other corner.

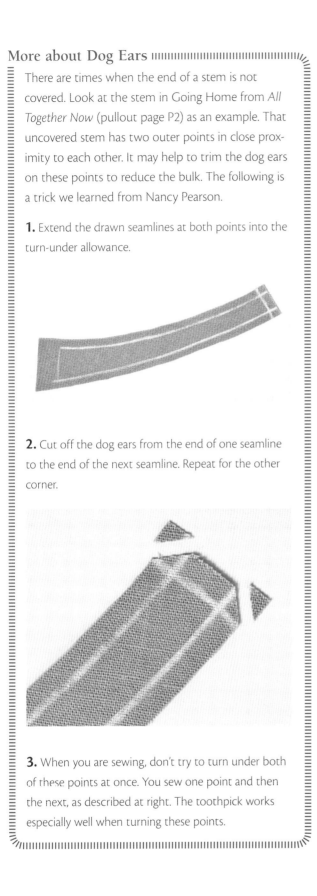

3. When you are sewing, don't try to turn under both of these points at once. You sew one point and then the next, as described at right. The toothpick works especially well when turning these points.

Sewing the First Side of the Outer Point

The turn-under allowance is bulky under a point. The fabric fills the point and pushes up. To hold the point firmly in place, you'll be shortening your stitches just before and just after the point, and you'll be using a tack stitch at the end of the first side.

1. Trace, cut, and finger-press your selected leaf as described in General Instructions (pages 19–22). When you finger-press, make sure to press the drawn line under with the turn-under allowance and finger-press beyond the end of the chalk lines into the seam allowance at the point. The finger-pressed creases cross each other.

2. Use the positioning overlay to place the appliqué piece on the block. Pin it in place.

Pinning Outer Points

The way you pin an outer point is very important. The pin at the point holds the point in place until you take the tack stitch. Refer to Pinning Outer Points (page 26) for instructions on how to pin outer points.

3. Sew toward the outer point. When you are ³⁄₁₆″ away from the point, begin taking shorter stitches, making the stitches closer together.

4. Sew until you are just inside the chalk line at the point. If you sew into the chalk line beyond the point, your chalk will show at the point.

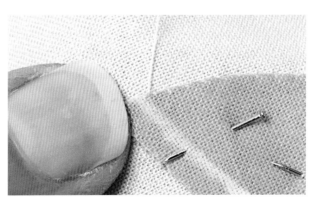

5. Place the needle into the background next to the appliqué, as if you were going to take another stitch, but instead come up again just inside the chalk line.

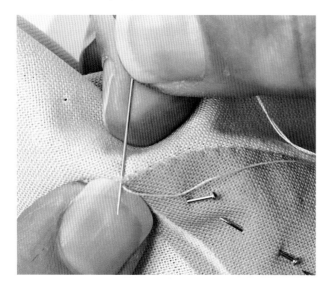

6. You are making a loop that you will pull tight to make a tack stitch.

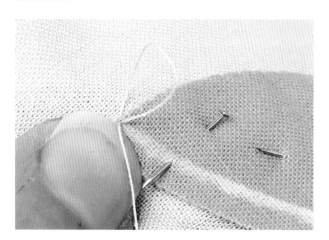

7. Pull the loop tight. That's your tack stitch! Do not turn the point until you have made the tack stitch.

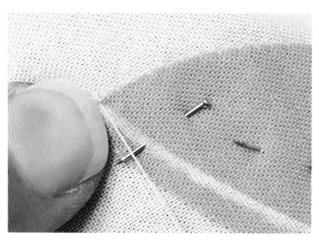

The Wooden Toothpick

Find your wooden toothpick and keep it handy! You'll be using it soon.

The toothpick works much better if it is damp but not wet. The moisture raises the grain of the wood so that it grabs the fabric better.

Turning an Outer Point Sewing Horizontally

1. With the first side sewn, remove the pin at the point. You don't need it anymore.

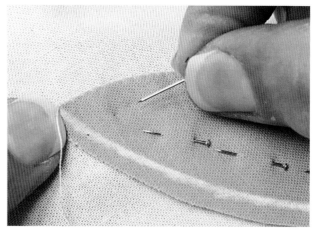

2. Turn the block in your hand so that you are in position to sew the second side of the point.

3. Park the needle off to the side out of your way. Pick up and dampen a toothpick. Place it *over* the fold in the turn-under allowance. The tip of the toothpick should be even with the cut edge of the seam allowance.

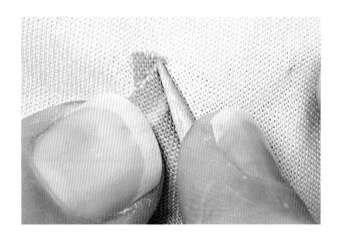

4. Push against fabric with the toothpick and rotate the turn-under allowance underneath the point. The toothpick should pivot on top of the tack stitch.

Imagine the way a windshield wiper moves. The tip of the toothpick moves in the same way, pivoting on top of the point.

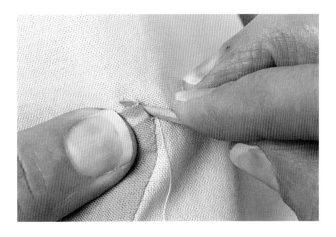
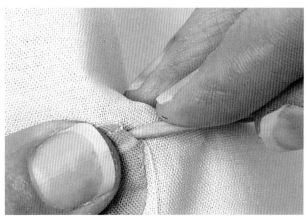

5. Rotate the toothpick only as far as the stitches on the first side of the point.

6. If you turned under a little more than you intended to, gently pull the thread out from the point to pop the point back out. You can do this anytime while turning the point. This maneuver takes some practice, but when mastered, the results are very good.

There Is Another Way

A more direct way of beginning to turn the fabric under at the outer point is to poke it under. The downside to this method is that you don't get as much of the fabric turned under the point to begin with, and it sometimes wads up at the point.

1. Place the point of the toothpick at the point of the turn-under allowance.

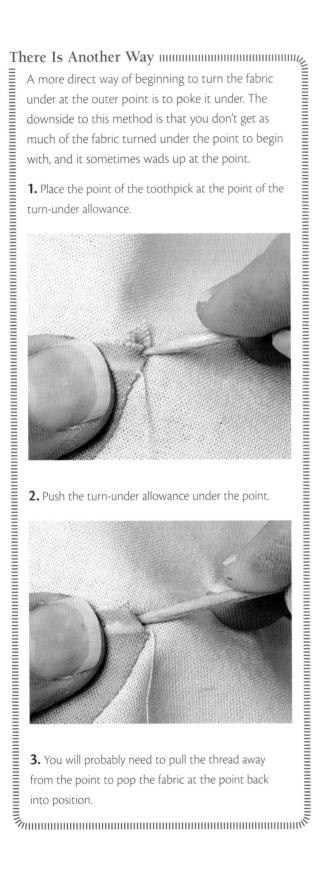

2. Push the turn-under allowance under the point.

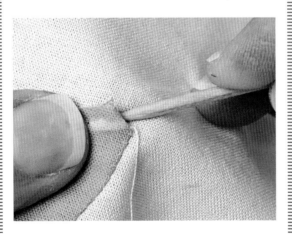

3. You will probably need to pull the thread away from the point to pop the fabric at the point back into position.

7. Bend your fingers so that you can reach under the point with the toothpick.

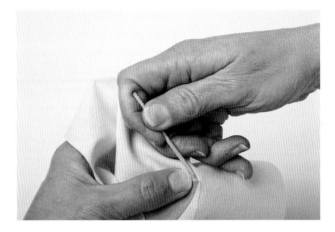

8. Use the toothpick to sweep the turn-under allowance away from the point so that it lies smooth.

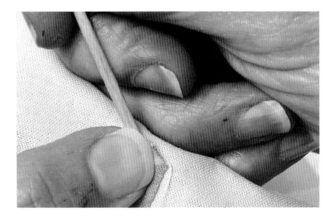

9. If you need to turn under more of the allowance, place the dampened toothpick next to the fold. Push against the fold and rotate more fabric under, again letting the toothpick pivot at the tack stitch.

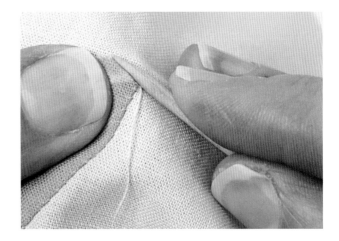

10. Reach underneath with the point of the toothpick and sweep the turn-under allowance away from the point, as you did in Step 8. *Never* scoop the turn-under allowance back *toward* the point—there is no room for more fabric at the point.

Continue in this manner, rotating fabric under the point and then sweeping it away from the point, until the chalk line is turned under and the turn-under allowance feels smooth under the point.

Do You Have a Point?

If you manage to turn the very tip of the point, just enough so that you can take one stitch, feel free to go ahead and take that one stitch. After that, you will continue working the turn-under allowance as described above.

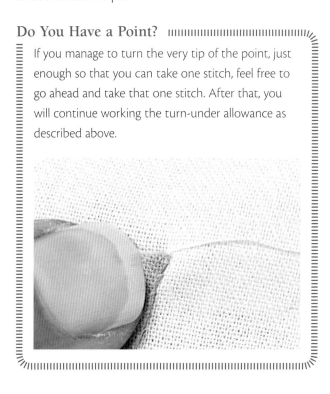

11. Stitch down the second side of the point. Remember to use shorter stitches for the first ³⁄₁₆˝ after the point. You can take only one stitch at a time. Don't try to work too far ahead.

Turning an Outer Point Sewing Vertically

1. With the first side stitched, make a tack stitch at the end of the point. Remove the pin at the point. You don't need it anymore.

2. Turn the block in your hand so that you are in position to sew the second side of the point.

Park the needle off to the side out of your way. Use the point of the toothpick to fold the point of the turn-under allowance under the point.

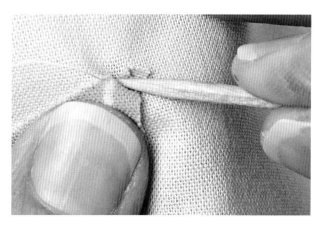

3. If you turned under a little more than you intended to, gently pull the thread out from the point to pop the point back out. You can do this anytime while turning the point.

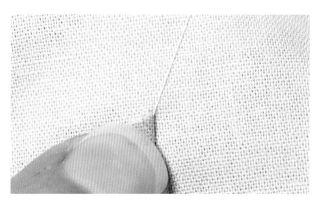

4. Reach underneath the point with a dampened toothpick and smooth the turn-under allowance away from the point.

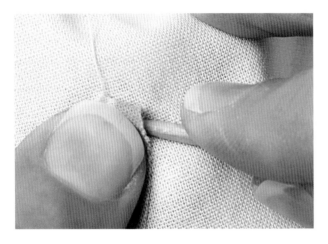

5. Place the dampened toothpick *over* the fold in the turn-under allowance. The tip of the toothpick should be even with the cut edge of the seam allowance.

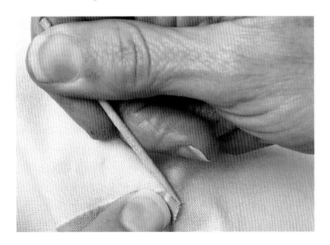

6. Push against the fabric with the toothpick and rotate the turn-under allowance underneath the point. The toothpick should pivot on top of the tack stitch.

Imagine the way a windshield wiper moves. The tip of the toothpick moves in the same way, pivoting on top of the point.

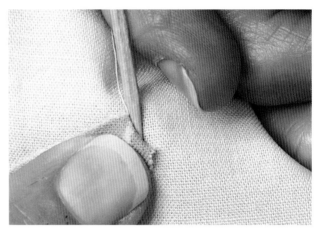

7. Rotate the toothpick only as far as the stitches on the first side of the point.

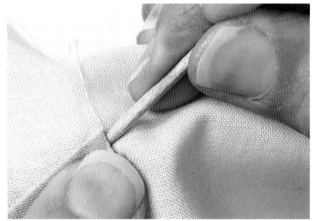

8. Place the point of the toothpick at the side of the point. Use the toothpick to smooth the turn-under allowance down and away from the point.

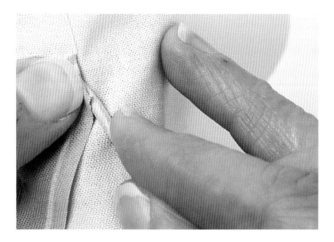

9. If you need to turn under more of the allowance, place the dampened toothpick next to the fold. Push against the fold and rotate more fabric under, again letting the toothpick pivot at the tack stitch.

10. Reach underneath with the point of the toothpick and sweep the turn-under allowance away from the point. *Never* push the turn-under allowance back *toward* the point—there is no room for more fabric at the point!

Continue in this manner, rotating fabric under the point and then sweeping it away from the point, until the chalk line is turned under.

11. Stitch down the second side of the point. Remember to use shorter stitches for the first ³⁄₁₆" after the point. You can take only one stitch at a time. Don't try to work too far ahead.

Inner Points

The problem with inner points is that they tend to fray because there is no turn-under allowance. We will show you how to sew inner points that are points (not curves) that do not fray. Slow down your stitching and give inner points your full attention, and you will be happy with the results.

Inner points are sewn the same way, regardless of the direction in which you stitch, with one exception noted in Step 6. To stitch along, use the scalloped flower from the Wreath block (pullout page P3).

1. Place the template on top of the selected fabric. Be sure to place the template on the fabric so that most of the edges will be on the diagonal grain of the fabric, unless you want to take advantage of a certain design in the fabric. Trace around the template.

2. Cut out the flower, leaving a ³⁄₁₆" turn-under allowance. Leave a bigger turn-under allowance at the base of the flower, where it will be covered by the flower center. *Do not clip the inner points at this time!*

3. *Finger-press*, making sure to press the drawn line to the back. Finger-press beyond the end of the chalk lines into the body of the appliqué piece at each inner point. The finger-pressed creases should cross each other.

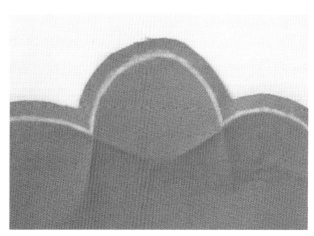

4. Use the positioning overlay to place the appliqué piece on the block. Pin it in place.

5. Sew toward the inner point. When you can no longer turn the turn-under allowance without distorting it, you must clip the inner point.

Your clip needs to be perfectly centered (see tip below). Clip to and just barely *through* the chalk line. The end of the clip should be at the finger-pressed crease.

How Do Scissors Work?

Think about this for a minute. The cut is made where the two scissor blades meet. When you put your scissors into the inner point to make a clip, you see only the top blade. Many quilters focus on the top blade, centering the whole blade without remembering that *the cut is made on the left side of the top blade*. Position the left side of the top scissor blade where you want the cut to be.

6. When sewing *horizontally*, you can use the needle or a toothpick to gently turn under the second side of the inner point along the finger-pressed line. This gets it out of the way. Do not do anything more than fold the second side of the point under.

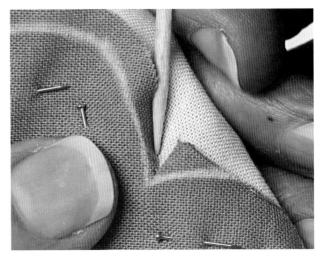

When sewing *vertically*, skip this step because your thumb is in the wrong place.

7. Use a dampened toothpick to gently *turn* the turn-under allowance on the first side of the inner point. Do not poke, scoop, twirl, or pull at the turn-under allowance at the inner point. Keep the toothpick parallel to the chalk line and gently tap the turn-under allowance. It will want to turn on the finger-pressed fold.

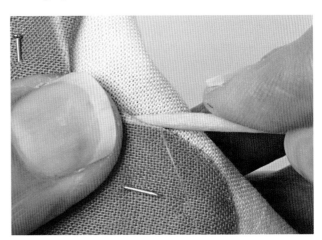

8. Continue stitching until you are within ³⁄₁₆″ of the point. *Gradually* begin making the stitches closer together and stitching farther and farther into the appliqué.

But My Stitches Will Show!

You have to catch more of the appliqué fabric at an inner point because if you don't, your fabric will fray. Yes, your stitches will show. However, your stitches will look good if

- they get bigger (and then smaller) gradually,

- they are perpendicular to the edge of the appliqué, and

- they are close together, but not so close as to resemble a satin stitch.

The stitches at the inner point should look like this:

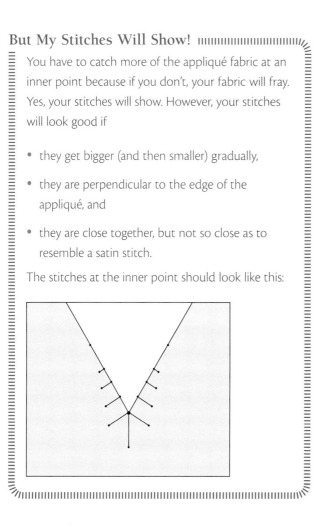

9. We like to make a tack stitch at the deepest part of the inner point. A tack stitch is a stitch in place. The needle goes into the background at the deepest part of the V and comes out exactly where the thread is coming out of the appliqué.

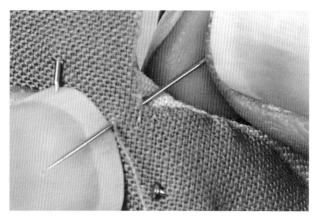

How Much Is Enough?

Some fabrics fray easily, while others don't fray much at all. Take your cue from the fabric. If you are appliquéing homespun fabric, the biggest stitch may need to be ⅛″ to keep the fabric from fraying. However, a batik will not fray much, so you can stay closer to the edge. The key to a successful inner point is to not let the fabric fray.

If the thread matches the appliqué fabric and your stitches *gradually* get bigger and then smaller, the thread will not be obvious. What people will notice is a sharp inner point that isn't fraying.

10. Work the second side of the inner point in the same manner. Make the stitches so they gradually move closer to the edge of the appliqué until you have a turn-under allowance again.

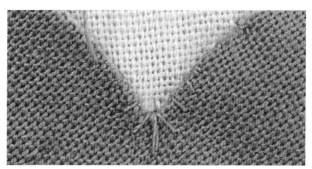

A finished inner point

Cutaway Appliqué

Cutaway appliqué is a technique that makes it easier to stitch shapes that are narrow, are very small, have multiple points, or would be hard to handle if cut out in the normal way. In this technique you cut out the appliqué piece with extra fabric around it, and then cut that extra fabric away as you stitch. You will use this technique again and again.

Pinning Narrow Shapes

When stitching a narrow shape, such as a stem, you need to decide which side of the shape to stitch first. When a shape is curved, sew the concave side first, if possible.

If you place pins down the *center* of a narrow appliqué piece, you'll have to remove the pin to make room for the turn-under allowance. When the pin is removed, the appliqué can shift out of position. Always place your pins ¼" away from, and parallel to, the edge that you will sew first, no matter how wide (or narrow) the shape.

As you can see in the photo below, the pins are very close to the line marking the second side of the stem. That's okay. These pins are in the correct position to sew the first side of the stem. When you are ready to sew the second side, remove the pins as you need to.

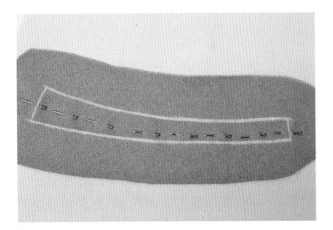

Cutaway on Narrow Shapes

Stems are the most common narrow shapes, but you should treat any long narrow shape as follows.

Note that the appliqué piece that you auditioned has likely been cut to size (page 13). You will need to cut a new shape with extra fabric around it to sew to the block.

1. Place the template on top of the selected fabric. Be sure that there is ¾"–1" of fabric all the way around the template. Place the template so that most of the edges will be on the diagonal grain of the fabric. Trace around the template.

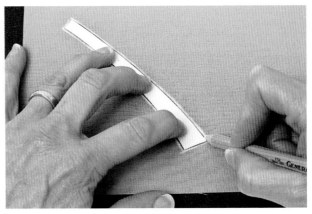

2. Cut out the appliqué piece, leaving ¾"–1" of excess fabric around the traced shape.

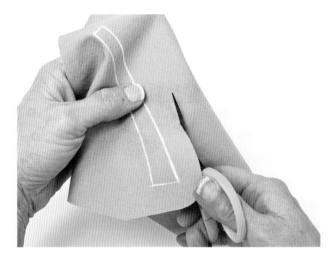

3. Finger-press as usual, making sure to finger-press the drawn line so that it does not show. Don't worry about the excess fabric; it will be cut off as you sew.

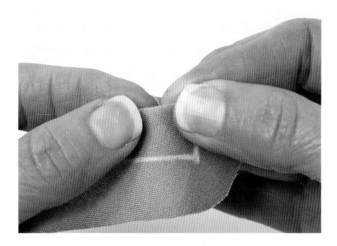

4. Use the vinyl overlay to position the appliqué piece on the block. Pin it in place.

5. Begin cutting away excess fabric from where you will start stitching, leaving a ³⁄₁₆" turn-under allowance.

Remember that the chalk line is part of the turn-under allowance. Cut away 2"–3" at a time.

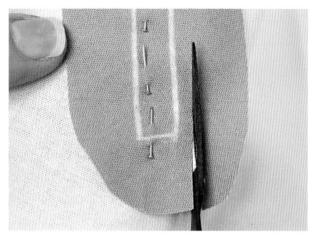

6. Bring the thread up inside the chalk mark at the end of the line and begin sewing. This is not an outer point that will be turned under. This is the end of the stem that will be covered by another piece. Never start at a point that must be turned under.

7. When you can no longer turn under the allowance without distorting the fabric, cut away more fabric. Feel free to cut off any of the excess fabric; it can be in the way when you stitch.

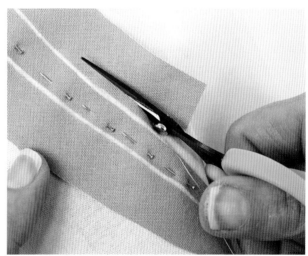

8. When you reach the end of the first side of the stem, knot your thread on the back. Sew the second side of the stem in the same manner.

Cutaway on Very Small Shapes

The problem with very small shapes is that they are hard to hold and impossible to pin in place. The trick to stitching very small shapes is to make them bigger, using the cutaway appliqué technique. We'll use a small circle from the Vase of Flowers block (pullout page P2) as an example.

Note that the appliqué piece that you auditioned has likely been cut to size. You will need to cut a new shape with extra fabric around it to sew to the block.

1. Place the template on top of the selected fabric. Trace around the template.

2. Cut out the appliqué piece, leaving 1″ or more of excess fabric around the traced shape. Finger-press as usual.

3. Use 2 pins to pin the appliqué in place. If you use only 1 pin, the piece can move out of position. Look closely at the pins in the photograph. They are near the side of the circle that will be sewn first, but there is still room for the turn-under allowance.

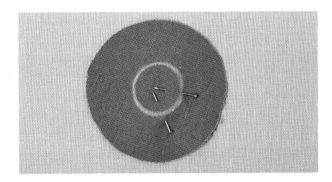

4. Begin cutting away excess fabric. On very small pieces, cut a *scant* 3/16″ turn-under allowance. However, don't cut your turn-under allowance so scant that it frays. Feel free to cut off the excess fabric.

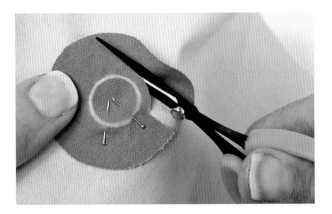

5. Begin stitching. You will have to trim away excess fabric often. Refer to Circles (page 59) for instructions on sewing circles.

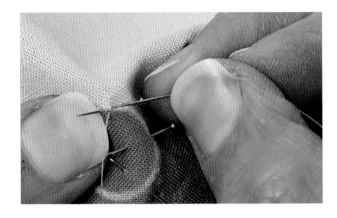

6. Sometimes it is easier to use a dampened toothpick to turn under these scant turn-under allowances.

7. Continue trimming and sewing until you have stitched all around the appliqué piece.

Cutaway on Shapes with Multiple Points

Tulips with pointed ends or five-point stars are typical shapes with several points. This book doesn't have any, but you see them often enough that we didn't want to ignore them. We'll use a tulip shape as an example.

The reason for using cutaway appliqué on these shapes is that the extra fabric helps to keep the points from moving out of position as you sew. Also, when you sew a shape with multiple points, the thread often hangs up on the points, causing them to fray. If the fabric is intact between the points, the thread has nothing to catch on, and the fabric at the point is more protected.

Note that the appliqué piece you auditioned has likely been cut to size. You will need to cut a new shape with extra fabric between the points to sew to the block.

1. Place the template on top of the selected fabric. Trace around the template.

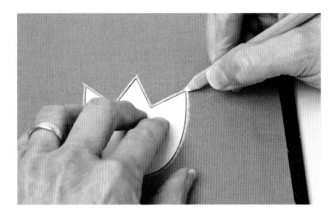

2. Cut out the appliqué piece. The rounded side of the tulip can be cut with a ³⁄₁₆″ turn-under allowance. Leave the fabric intact between the points. Finger-press as usual.

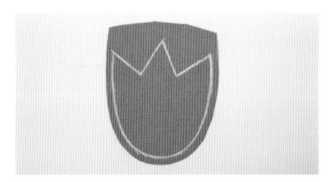

3. Begin sewing at the base of the tulip. Make a tack stitch at the end of the first side of the point. Refer to Outer Points (page 42) for instructions on sewing outer points.

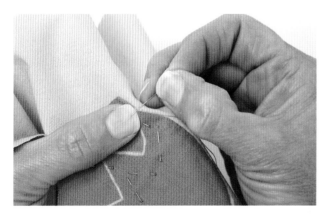

4. Cut away the V of fabric. The turn-under allowance will be more uniform if you cut in toward the inner point from both directions. Do not clip the inner point until necessary. Refer to Inner Points (page 49) for instructions on sewing inner points.

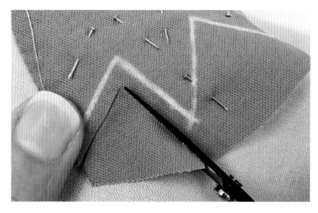

5. Continue sewing, trimming fabric away from between the points as necessary.

Five-Point Stars

Just in case you were wondering, a five-point star would be cut out as shown.

Finger-press and pin the star in place. Cut away one V of fabric between two points. Begin sewing on a flat area between an outer and inner point.

Curves and Circles

When you think of pieced quilts, you think of straight lines. Appliqué quilts, however, are full of lovely curves and round circles. This curviness is what sets appliqué quilts apart from most pieced quilts. Inner curves, outer curves, and circles are easy to do if you take your time—and know the tricks!

Inner Curves

Inner curves must be clipped. The edge of an inner curve can fray more easily because of the clips. To prevent fraying, make the stitches a little bit closer together and a little bit deeper into the appliqué fabric. Make sure the thread matches the appliqué fabric so that these deeper stitches are not obvious.

We'll use an inner curve from the large flower in the Passionate Flower block (pullout page P1).

1. Under normal circumstances, you would place the template on top of the selected applique fabric so that most of the edges are on the diagonal grain of the fabric (page 19). In this case, though, we're doing reverse appliqué (page 65), so this template is placed on the block background fabric.

2. Finger-press a series of short, overlapping straight lines to create an inner curve.

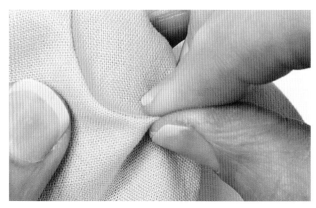

3. For reverse appliqué, cut away the center area *after* finger pressing and pinning. Use a ³⁄₁₆″ turn-under allowance. Begin sewing. When you reach an inner curve and can no longer turn under the allowance without distorting the fabric, it is time to clip. Turn the work so that you are not cutting at an awkward angle. Make as many clips as necessary to ensure a smooth curve. Make each clip perpendicular to the chalk line.

Clipping Inner Curves

- When you have to clip an inner curve, *always* make a minimum of three clips to ensure a smooth curve. The first clip should be at the deepest part of the curve. Make at least one clip on either side of the first clip. Beyond that, clip as many times as necessary for a smooth curve.

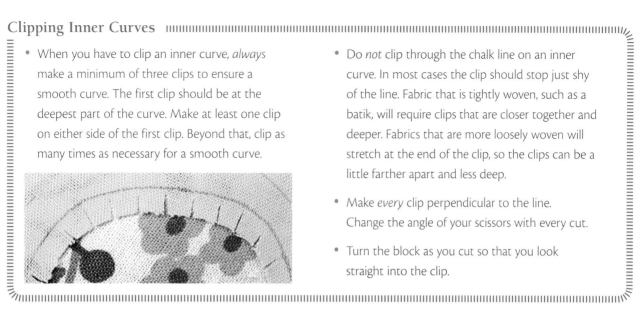

- Do *not* clip through the chalk line on an inner curve. In most cases the clip should stop just shy of the line. Fabric that is tightly woven, such as a batik, will require clips that are closer together and deeper. Fabrics that are more loosely woven will stretch at the end of the clip, so the clips can be a little farther apart and less deep.

- Make *every* clip perpendicular to the line. Change the angle of your scissors with every cut.

- Turn the block as you cut so that you look straight into the clip.

4. Do not turn under one segment at a time. That can cause the fabric at the end of the clip to fray. Make a sweep with the side of your toothpick, beginning at the far end of the inner curve.

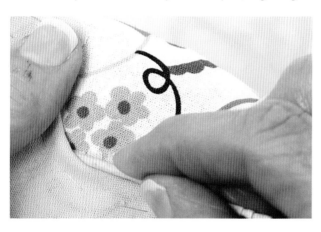

5. Work back toward your last stitch. The turn-under allowance will turn under along the finger-pressed crease.

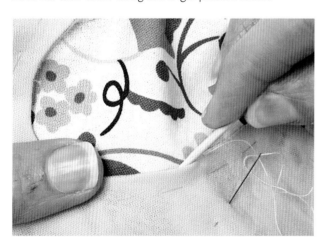

6. When most of the turn-under allowance is turned under, stitch the edge in place with an invisible stitch. Use the toothpick to sweep under more of the turn-under allowance as necessary.

Clipping can cause the turn-under allowance to be weaker, which is why your stitches need to be a little closer together.

Stitches in an inner curve need to catch a little more of the appliqué fabric than normal because if you come up at the base of a clip, the fabric can fray. How much more fabric you need to catch depends on the weave of the fabric (page 51, How Much Is Enough). If your stitches are of a uniform size, they won't be noticeable.

Outer Curves

Outer curves are tricky because the turn-under allowance can pleat, making points in what should be a smooth curve. How do you stop these pleats and points?

Make sure the turn-under allowance is no bigger than ³⁄₁₆″. Sometimes a curve turns easier if you leave a *scant* ³⁄₁₆″ turn-under allowance. However, if the turn-under allowance is too small, the fabric will fray, making it harder to turn.

You can turn under and control only *one stitch at a time*! Often you can avoid pleats entirely by turning under only enough for one stitch.

When pleats do form, take the time to work the pleats out. Never clip an outer curve!

We'll use a leaf from the Cotton Flowers block (pullout page P3) to show outer curves.

1. Place the template on top of the selected fabric so that most of the edges will be on the diagonal grain of the fabric. Trace around the template.

2. Cut out the shape, leaving a ³⁄₁₆″ turn-under allowance.

3. Finger-press a series of short, overlapping straight lines to create an outer curve. You will probably be able to use the fingers from only one hand to finger-press an outer curve.

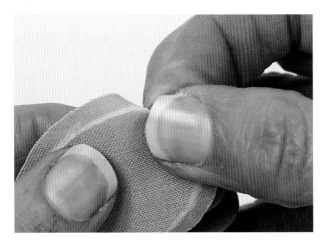

4. Use the positioning overlay to position the appliqué piece on the block. Pin it in place.

5. Begin sewing. When you reach the curve, you can turn and control only *one stitch* at a time. Use the point of the needle to grab the middle of the turn-under allowance underneath the edge.

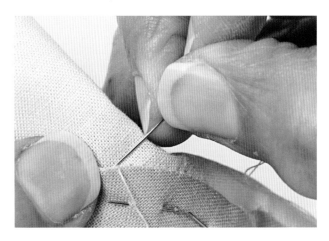

6. Then gently move the turn-under allowance into place. This is effective but requires that you be patient enough to turn under only enough fabric to take one stitch.

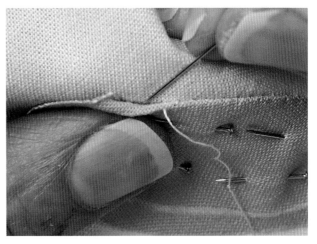

Why Do My Curves Have Points?

When you turn under too much of the allowance on an outer curve, a pleat will form. Where you have a pleat, you will see a point at the outer edge of the appliqué. You can feel the pleat with your fingers.

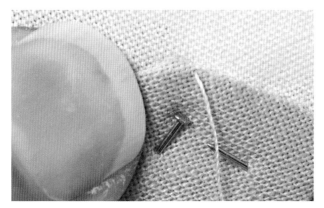

1. *Always* take the time to open a pleat and smooth it out. Reach into the pleat with either a damp toothpick or your needle.

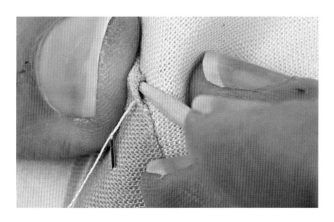

2. Sweep the fabric in the pleat to the right.

3. Take out the toothpick and reinsert it behind the pleat. Sweep the fabric in the pleat to the left.

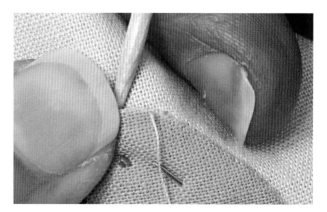

4. Continue smoothing out the fabric in the pleat until it is no longer bunched up—you should be able to feel it with your fingers. The point at the edge will smooth out.

5. After you smooth out the pleat, continue stitching. When another pleat forms, repeat the process.

6. If your curve flattens out, use your needle to lift the edge, rounding it out. Outer curves are very pretty if you take the time to do them well.

Circles

Once you have learned how to needle-turn a lovely outer curve, you can use the same technique on circles because a circle is a continuous outer curve. The most common problem with circles is the pleats that make your circles pointy. We just showed you how to avoid or fix these pleats above.

That said, there are some additional techniques that will help you make lovely needle-turned circles.

1. Place the template on top of the selected fabric. Trace around the template.

2. Cut out circles with a ³⁄₁₆″ turn-under allowance.

3. Finger-press a series of short, overlapping straight lines to create an outer curve. You will probably be able to use the fingers from only one hand to finger-press an outer curve. Do not finger-press any points or flat areas into your circle.

4. Use the positioning overlay to place the circle on the block. Use at least 2 pins (and more if necessary) when pinning a circle. This will keep the circle from shifting during stitching.

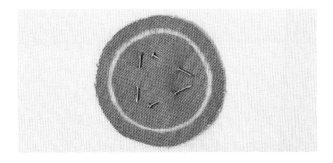

5. Bring the needle up through the finger-pressed fold. Most of the time you turn under the turn-under allowance for the first stitch you will take. But if you do that on a circle, you are likely to have a point when you sew around the circle and back to your first stitch.

It works better to turn under both the first and last stitch when you begin sewing on an outer curve.

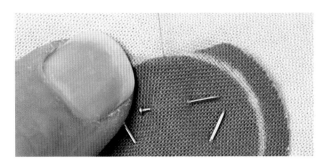

6. Begin sewing. Remember, you can turn under and control only *one stitch at a time!* Often, you can avoid pleats entirely by turning under only enough fabric for one stitch.

7. Stitch around the circle until you are about ³⁄₁₆" from the first stitch. The turn-under allowance will look like a triangle sticking out from the edge of the circle.

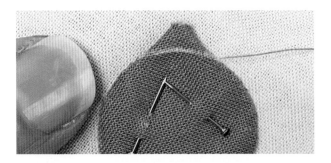

8. Turn under the remaining turn-under allowance. This will form a flat space with a pleat at either end.

9. Use your needle or a dampened toothpick to fan open the first pleat.

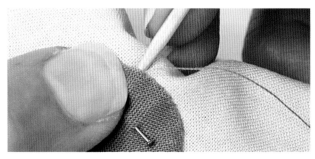

10. Often the flattened area rounds out as you open the pleat. If it doesn't, use the tip of the needle to reach under the flattened edge of the circle and gently pull the edge out until round.

11. Sew until you reach the last pleat. Use the needle or a dampened toothpick to fan the pleat open. Finish sewing the circle.

Tip
We love using Karen Kay Buckley's Perfect Circles as templates to trace around.

Off-the-Block Construction

Sometimes it is easier to sew appliqué pieces together "off-the-block" and then sew them as a unit to the block. When working off-the-block, you most often work from the top down—rather than from the bottom up, as you do when sewing appliqué pieces onto the block itself. As you will see, this is a handy technique to use in a variety of situations.

Simple Off-the-Block Construction

Choose this technique when appliqué pieces are stacked on top of each other, as the circles are in the Lollipops block (pullout page P4). Notice that the stem lies over multiple circles in the two flowers on the left. In this case the bottom three circles can be sewn together off-the-block. In the flower on the right, the top three circles can be sewn off-the-block.

When stitching off-the-block, it is difficult to work with pieces of fabric that are too small. The shape on the bottom needs to be bigger than it will be when sewn to the block. Anything much smaller than 5″ × 5″ is hard to hold on to while you sew.

As is true in the cutaway appliqué technique, the appliqué shape that you cut to size and auditioned on your design wall will not be used.

The following example uses the flower on the right, templates #7, #8, and #9.

1. Choose the fabric for each of the 3 shapes. Cut a 7″ × 7″ square of fabric for #7. Cut a 6″ × 6″ square of fabric for #8. Place the appropriate template in the center of each square and trace around it. Do not cut the #7 and #8 shapes yet.

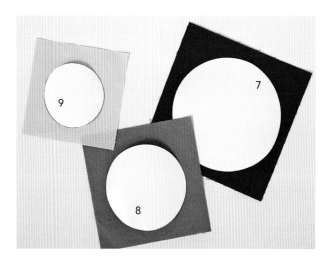

Place the #9 template on the fabric you have chosen and trace around it. Cut it out with a scant 3⁄16″ seam allowance.

2. Finger-press #9. Use the positioning overlay to place it on top of #8. Pin and then stitch it in place. Press the unit if needed. Trim away the excess fabric, leaving a ³⁄₁₆″ turn-under allowance.

3. Finger-press the outer edge. Use the positioning overlay to place it on top of #7. Pin and then stitch it in place.

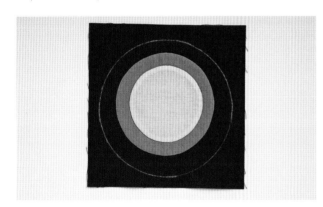

4. Turn over the #7/8/9 unit. If you want to trim away the excess fabric behind the smaller circles, now is your chance. You don't have to, but you can if you like. Be sure to leave a ³⁄₁₆″ seam allowance.

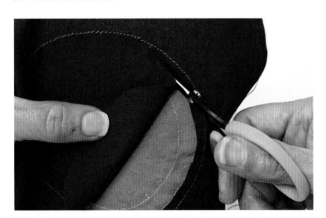

5. Trim the excess fabric from the #7/8/9 unit, leaving a ³⁄₁₆″ turn-under allowance. Finger-press the outer edge. Use the positioning overlay to place it on the block in the correct stitching sequence.

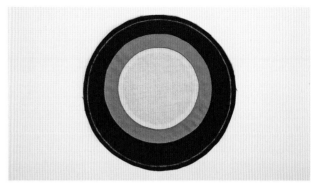

More Complex Off-the-Block Construction

Look at the flower centers on the Wreath block (pullout page P3). They are all the same even though they are numbered differently. In this block you can choose to sew one big scalloped flower, or you can sew five different petals in each quadrant. The number sequence changes depending on which flower type you choose. In this section, we will use numbers 6–10.

The bottom oval, #6, is cut from one piece of fabric. The strips, #7–10, and the circle, #11, are sewn to the #6 oval off-the-block. This is the best way to sew this flower center.

1. Choose the fabric for each shape. Cut a 5″ × 5″ square of fabric for #6. Place the template in the center of this square and trace around it.

Place the remaining templates on the appropriate fabric and trace around them. Cut them out with a ³⁄₁₆″ turn-under allowance. Leave extra turn-under allowance at each end of these shapes.

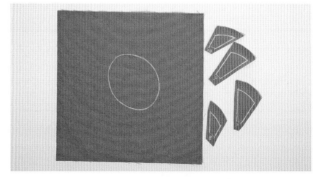

2. Finger-press the sides of #7. Use the positioning overlay to place it on top of #6. Pin and then stitch it in place.

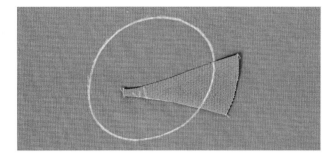

3. Finger-press, pin, and stitch the remaining pieces to #6 in sequence. Press the unit if needed.

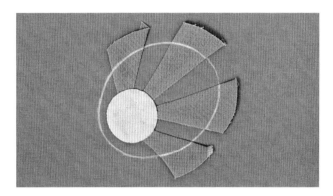

4. Trim the excess fabric from the #6–11 unit, leaving a ³⁄₁₆″ turn-under allowance.

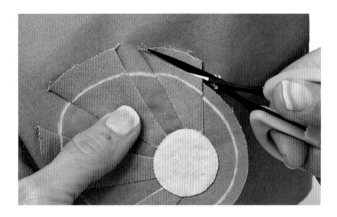

Finger-press the outer edge, paying special attention to the areas where the fabric is doubled. Use the positioning overlay to place it on the block in the correct stitching sequence.

Rather than changing thread colors when we stitch around this shape, we look for the thread color that is the least visible on both fabrics.

Two-Part Leaves

Leaves that are made up of two parts are easier to stitch together off-the-block. Work from the top down, just as you did for off-the-block construction. *Follow these instructions carefully; don't trace or cut out the piece on the bottom until the top fabric has been sewn to it.*

We'll work on leaf #1/2 from the Leaves block (pullout page P1).

1. Choose the 2 fabrics that make up the leaf. Place the #2 template on top of the appropriate fabric. Be sure to place the template on the fabric so that most of the edges will be on the diagonal grain of the fabric. Trace around the template.

Cut out piece #2, leaving a ³⁄₁₆″ turn-under allowance. Leave a bigger turn-under allowance where the stem will cover the base of the leaf. Finger-press the vein side of piece #2 (where it will meet piece #1).

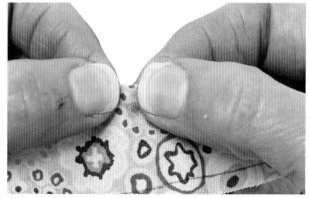

2. Cut out an 8″ × 8″ square of the #1 fabric. Pin the finger-pressed #2 piece to the #1 fabric on the diagonal grain of the fabric.

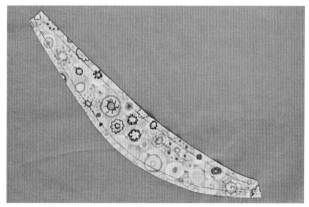

Use the Positioning Overlay if Needed ⫿⫿⫿⫿⫿

You have not yet drawn the #1 shape onto the #1 fabric. When you place the #2 piece on the #1 fabric, be sure to leave room for the other side of the leaf, including the turn-under allowance. You may need to use the overlay to be sure that you are leaving enough fabric for the #1 side of the leaf.

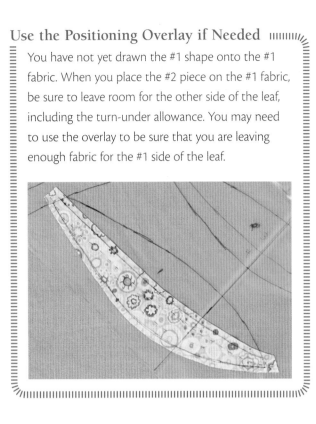

3. Stitch appliqué piece #2 to the #1 fabric along the vein of the leaf. Do not sew beyond the drawn lines at either end of the leaf.

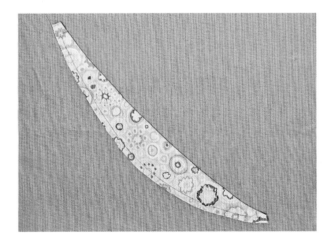

4. Place the #1 template next to the sewn vein. Trace around the outer edge to form the rest of the leaf.

5. Cut away the excess fabric from around the leaf, leaving a ³⁄₁₆″ turn-under allowance.

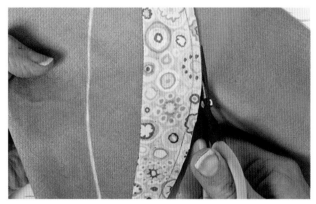

6. Turn over the leaf and trim away the excess fabric under #2, leaving a ³⁄₁₆″ seam allowance.

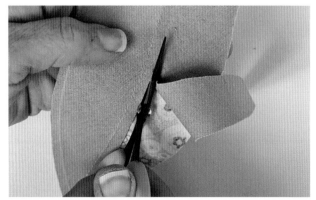

7. Finger-press the leaf. Use the positioning overlay to place it on the block. Pin and stitch the leaf in place.

Reverse Appliqué

For the most part, appliqué shapes are stitched *on top* of a block. In reverse appliqué, however, you cut through the fabric on top to reveal the fabric that is *below* it. Reverse appliqué is often stitched off-the-block (page 61).

Many quilters think that reverse appliqué is hard, but it's not. As you follow the instructions, you'll see that reverse appliqué is easy! The trick is to leave the bottom fabric *big*. Don't cut the bottom fabric to size until your reverse appliqué is done.

Why Reverse Appliqué?

When you stitch appliqué pieces to a block, they are on top of the block. The shapes come forward in space. They have dimension. Reverse-appliquéd shapes push back into the block, creating depth. Use reverse appliqué on shapes that recede into other shapes—such as windows and doors in houses. You might also reverse appliqué eyes so that animals (or people) don't look bug-eyed.

Reverse Appliqué a Window and Door

Look at the Going Home block (pullout page P2). Windows #14, #21, and #24 are reverse appliquéd, as is door #15. Let's concentrate on window #14.

1. Cut an 8″ × 8″ square of fabric for house shape #16. Place the template on the diagonal grain of the fabric, unless there is a design in the fabric that dictates a different placement. Trace around the template and inside the window and door openings.

2. Finger-press the traced lines for the window and door. Remember to turn the chalk line to the inside of the window and door. You should not see the chalk line on top of the house.

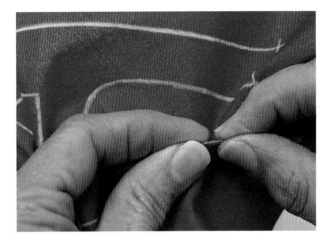

3. Cut a 4″ × 4″ square of fabric for the #14 window. Place the window fabric right side up underneath the house fabric, centered behind the window. Pin or baste it in place. Be sure that your pins are ¼″ away from, and parallel to, the edges of the window.

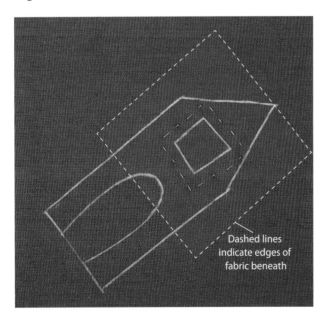

Dashed lines indicate edges of fabric beneath

Always, Always, Always! Always cut the fabric that is underneath—the one that will be revealed—bigger than it needs to be. It is very difficult to try to reverse appliqué onto a tiny bitty piece of fabric.

4. Cut out the fabric in the center of the #16 window, leaving a ³⁄₁₆″ turn-under allowance. Cut *through **only** the top fabric.*

Do not cut out the window *before* you pin it, because it is too easy to pull or stretch the larger piece out of shape if it has a hole in it.

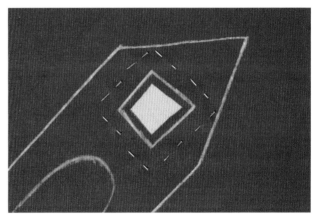

5. Begin stitching in the center of any side of the window. Clip and sew inner points (page 49) as necessary.

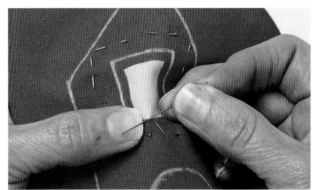

6. Turn the appliqué over and trim away the excess fabric, leaving a ³⁄₁₆″ allowance.

7. Cut a 4″ × 5″ rectangle of fabric for the #15 door. Place it right side up underneath the house fabric, centered behind the door. Pin or baste it in place. Be sure that your pins are ¼″ away from, and parallel to, the edge of the door.

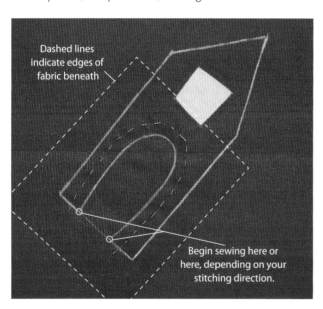

Dashed lines indicate edges of fabric beneath

Begin sewing here or here, depending on your stitching direction.

8. Begin trimming away the excess house fabric from the bottom edge of the door, stopping after you have cut 2″–3″ down the inside of the door. Only the sides and top of this door are reverse appliquéd. The bottom of the door is turned under with the bottom of #15. Begin sewing at the same place you began trimming.

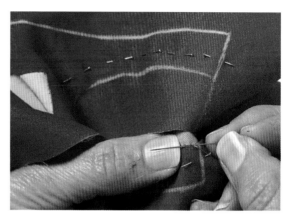

9. Continue in this manner, cutting away more fabric as necessary, until the door is stitched. Turn the block over and trim away the excess door fabric, leaving a ³⁄₁₆″ allowance.

Reverse Appliqué a Flower Center

Look at the numbers on the flower centers in the Cotton Flowers block (pullout page P3). Notice that the numbers on the flower centers are lower than those on the flowers. That tells you that they are reverse appliquéd. That said, if you choose to appliqué the flower centers on top of the flowers, you can. The next page shows how to use reverse appliqué.

1. Cut a 4" × 5" rectangle of fabric for flower #6. Place the template on the diagonal grain of the fabric, unless there is a design in the fabric that dictates a different placement. Trace around the template and inside the flower center opening.

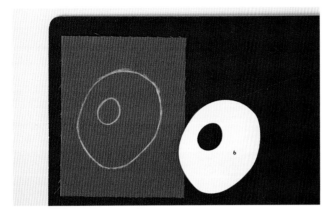

2. Finger-press the traced lines for the flower center. Remember to turn the chalk line to the inside of the flower center. You should not see the chalk line on top of the flower.

3. Cut a 3" × 3" square of fabric for the flower center. Place this fabric right side up underneath the flower fabric, centered behind the flower center. Pin or baste it in place. Be sure that your pins are ¼" away from, and parallel to, the edge of the flower center.

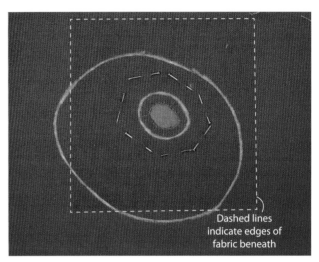

Dashed lines indicate edges of fabric beneath

4. Cut out the fabric in the middle of the flower center, leaving a ³⁄₁₆" turn-under allowance. Cut *through only the top fabric.*

5. Clip the inner curve (page 56) all the way around the flower center. Use a dampened toothpick to turn the turn-under allowance. Begin stitching between clips at the flattest part of the curve.

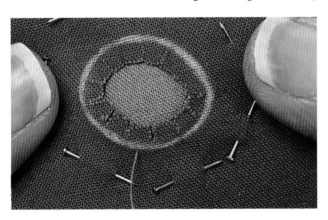
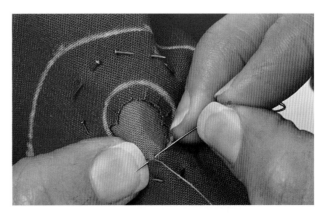

6. After the flower center is stitched, turn the appliqué over and trim away the excess flower center fabric, leaving a ³⁄₁₆" allowance.

Appliqué with Attitude Stitches

An appliqué stitch with attitude is one that is both very visible and decorative in its own right. In our book *Appliqué with Attitude*, we show a running stitch, a mock blanket stitch, and a serrated stitch variation. In this book we concentrate on the running stitch.

Detail from *Pretty Perky* (page 93)

We use Prescencia's perle cotton in either size 12 or size 16. Size 12 is a little thicker and therefore more visible. Size 16 is thinner and pulls through the fabric a little easier.

Bohin's size 9 crewel needle works with both of these weights of perle cotton. If you need a needle threader, we found one that works with these perle cottons and this needle—it is the Quilter's Needle Threader by Collins.

Running Stitch

The running stitch will feel familiar to those of you who have hand quilted. The stitches create a dashed line that accentuates the edge of the appliqué.

1. Prepare the appliqué pieces in exactly the same way as you would for the invisible stitch. Finger-press the shape (page 22) and pin it to the block.

2. Bring the needle up through the appliqué fabric about 1/16" inside the finger-pressed crease that is at the inside edge of the drawn line. Use the needle to turn under the turn-under allowance; hold it in place with the finger and thumb of your holding hand. The knot and the thread tail will be buried under the appliqué.

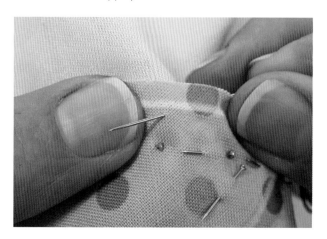

About the Running Stitch

The stitch length, and the space between each stitch, should be ⅟₁₆″–⅛″ long. Your needle will follow the edge of your appliqué and be about ⅟₁₆″ away from it.

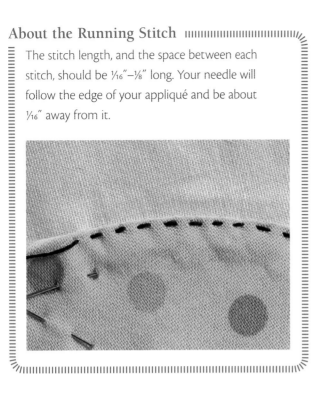

3. Stitch from right to left (if you are right-handed). Hold the block so that the edge of the appliqué is running from side to side. Your left thumb should be sitting directly on top of the folded edge and be positioned so that when you stitch, the needle is pointed at the end of your thumb, not at the side of your thumb.

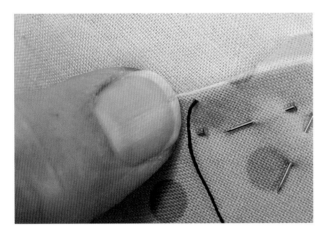

4. Place the needle a stitch's length to the left of the point where you brought up the thread. Poke the needle straight down through the appliqué and the background until you hit the tip of your underneath finger.

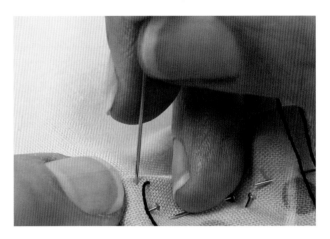

5. Rock over your underneath finger and push the needle back up through the background and the folded edge of the appliqué. Try to make the stitches and spaces between them uniform. Really bend over the bottom finger so that your needle travels as straight as it can up through the layers. Keep pinching the fabric together with your left finger and thumb to keep the layers together and to help you make the stitch length you prefer.

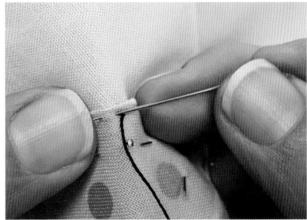

6. Unless your fabric is very tightly woven, you can pack 2–4 stitches on your needle at a time. Push the needle up only the length of 1 stitch and then point it right back down through the layers until you can feel it with your bottom finger.

7. Push the needle down until it feels like you have gone the distance you want to go, and then bend it back up over your bottom finger.

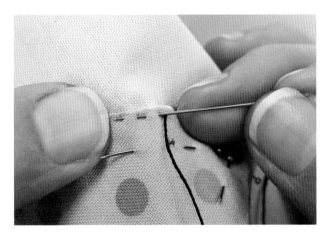

8. When you think you have all the stitches you can make on the needle, pull the needle and thread through the fabric. Don't pull the thread so tight that you pleat your edges, but don't leave the thread loose either.

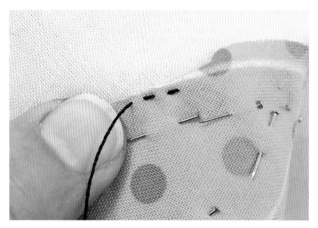

9. Continue in this manner, turning under the edges along the finger-pressed crease, and rocking the needle up and down to make your stitches.

Ending a Running Stitch

Because your first running stitch is brought up through only the appliqué, the beginning of that stitch is not held tightly to the background. Some shapes you will stitch all the way around until you are back to your first stitch. In these cases we stitch over our first stitch with our last stitch.

Continuous Bias

Fabric strips cut on the bias are stretchy. These stretchy strips are perfect for binding, bias stems, and piping and cording. Make a continuous bias strip when you need more than a short length of bias—a surprisingly small square of fabric makes quite a bit of bias, and there is almost no waste.

Bias binding wears better than straight binding at the edge of a quilt because the folded edge is on the bias grain of the fabric.

Bias from a Square

For binding, we normally cut our strips 2½″ wide. This strip is pressed in half lengthwise, wrong sides together. The raw edges are sewn even with the quilt top, and the folded edge is turned to the back and stitched by hand or machine over the raw edges of the quilt (Sewing Binding to the Quilt, page 76).

1. Start with a square of fabric and cut it in half diagonally. Refer to the project instructions for the size of the square.

2. Sew the 2 triangles right sides together, as shown. Be sure that these edges are on the straight of grain. If you are using striped fabric, match the stripes. You may need to offset the fabric a little to make the stripes match.

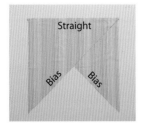

3. Press the seam allowances open. Make a short cut 2½″ wide into each side as shown. Cuts are always made on the bias grain of the fabric. Check the grain line before you cut.

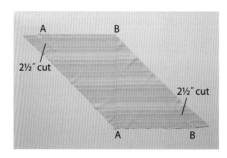

4. Match the A's and B's with the fabric right sides together. Pin and sew the fabric (from A to B) to make a tube. Press the seam open.

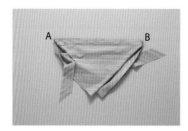

5. Use a rotary cutter and ruler to cut the continuous bias strip 2½" wide.

Cutting Tip for Continuous Bias

Try putting a small cutting mat on the end of an ironing board. Slide the tube of fabric over the mat. Use a ruler and rotary cutter to cut a long strip of continuous bias, rotating the tube of fabric as needed.

Cut using gentle pressure. If the ironing board is padded, the cutting surface may give if you press too hard.

6. Press the binding strip in half lengthwise, wrong sides together.

Bias from Strips

When you don't need a very long length of continuous bias binding, it can be easier to make it from strips rather than from a fabric tube.

1. Cut several strips from a single layer of fabric on the bias at the designated width. Angle both ends at the same 45° angle.

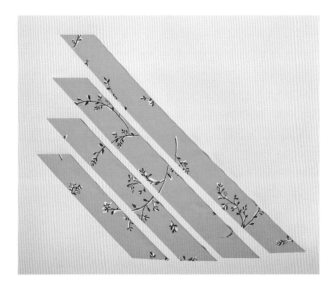

2. Place 2 strips right sides together. Offset the ends so that a V is formed at the ¼" seamline. Sew together.

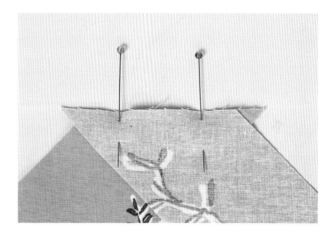

3. Continue sewing strips together, end-to-end, with a ¼" seam. Press the seams open. Trim away the dog ears that extend beyond the edges of the strips.

4. Press the binding strip in half lengthwise, wrong sides together.

Bias Stems

We use this technique for stems that are uniform in width. It is also good for very long stems or vines. We used bias stems in the borders in *The Garden at My House* (page 84).

To make these bias stems, you will need a package of bias bars. Each package contains a variety of bar widths. We like heat-resistant plastic bars. Metal Celtic bars work the same way.

Tip

When making bias stems, press seam allowances in one direction—not open.

1. Make a continuous bias strip 1½″ wide (pages 72–73). Press the strip in half lengthwise, wrong sides together.

2. Place the folded edge of the bias strip along the correct line on the seam guide of the sewing machine. (For example, for ⅜″ stems use the ⅜″ line.) Before you sew too far, insert the bias bar into the open end to make sure it fits. Sew the length of the bias strip.

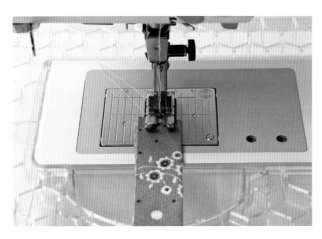

3. Trim away the excess fabric, leaving a very scant seam allowance.

4. Insert the appropriate size bias bar into the sewn bias tube. Shift the seam to the back of the bar and press it in place. Move the bias bar down the tube, pressing as you go.

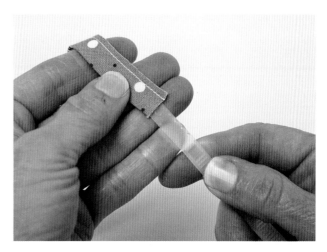

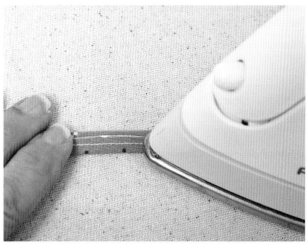

5. Hold up the finished bias stem. Notice that it curves more in one direction than the other. The side closest to the seamline makes the tighter curve. When possible, match this side of the bias stem to the concave side of the stem on the pattern.

Finishing the Quilt

Backing, Layering, and Quilting

1. Assemble the quilt top following the instructions for each project.

2. Construct the back of the quilt, piecing as needed.

3. Place the backing right side down on a firm surface. Tape it down to keep it from moving around while you baste, but do not stretch the backing out of shape.

4. Place the batting over the backing and pat out any wrinkles. Do not stretch the batting out of shape by smoothing or stroking it.

5. Center the quilt top right side up over the batting.

6. Baste together the layers. Yes, we thread baste for both hand and machine quilting. Baste side to side and top to bottom.

7. Quilt by machine or by hand.

Here's a Trick!

Trim the batting so that it extends 1″ beyond the edge of the quilt top on each side. Trim the backing so that it extends 1″ beyond the batting. Fold the backing fabric over the batting. The raw edges of the back and the quilt top will meet. Baste the folded backing fabric in place over the batting.

This simple step keeps the edges of your quilt from stretching out of shape whether you quilt by hand or machine.

8. Trim the outer edges, leaving ¼″ of backing and batting extending beyond the edge of the quilt top. This extra fabric and batting will fill the binding nicely.

If you are going to mark quilting lines, do so lightly before you layer and baste the three layers together. We use the same pencils that we use in our appliqué (page 7). Test your pencil on scrap fabric to make sure it will come out later.

Never heat set a mark into your quilt! Do not iron over a mark that you want to remove later. Be careful how you handle your quilt in progress. Never leave it in a hot car for any length of time.

Use the best equipment that you can afford. When hand quilting, the best equipment means having a good hoop or frame. Choose a thimble that is comfortable. As your hands change with time, keep your thimble up to date.

Successful machine quilting requires the best sewing machine and table that you can afford. We each love machine quilting on our Sweet Sixteen made by Handi Quilter. Quilting gloves allow you to move the quilt without so much strain on your hands. A Teflon Supreme Slider helps the quilt slide easily on the bed of the machine. Use good thread and change your needle often.

9. Finish the outer edges with continuous bias binding (page 72).

Sewing Binding to the Quilt

Refer to Continuous Bias (page 72) to make enough bias strips to bind your quilt. To determine the length of the strip you need, measure the perimeter of your quilt and add 18" for the mitered corners and the overlap.

1. Be sure the outer edges of the quilt are trimmed (page 75).

2. Open the binding to a single layer and cut the first end of the binding at a 45° angle. Turn under this end ½" and press. Refold the binding in half lengthwise.

3. With the raw edges even, pin the binding to the edge of the quilt top, beginning a few inches away from a corner.

Start sewing 6" from the beginning of the binding strip, using a ¼" seam allowance and the walking foot.

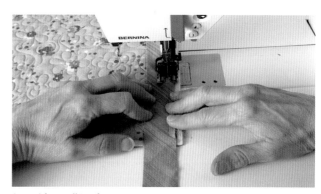

Sew with a walking foot.

4. Stop ¼" away from the corner and backstitch several stitches.

5. Fold the binding straight up as shown. Note the 45° angle.

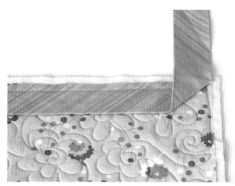

Fold binding up.

6. Fold the binding straight down and begin sewing the next side of the quilt.

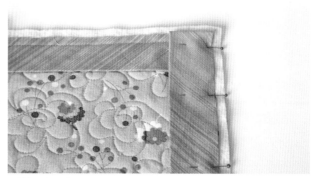

Fold binding down and sew.

7. Sew the binding to all 4 sides of the quilt, following the process in Steps 4–6. Stop a few inches before you reach the beginning of the binding, but don't trim the excess binding yet.

8. Overlap the ends of the binding, and cut the second end at a 90° angle. Be sure to cut the binding long enough so that the cut end is covered completely by the angled end.

9. Slip the 90° end into the angled end.

Slip 90° end into angled end.

10. Pin the joined ends to the quilt and finish sewing the binding to the quilt.

Pin joined ends and finish sewing.

11. Turn the binding to the back of the quilt, covering the raw edges. If there is too much batting, trim some to leave the binding nicely filled. Hand stitch the folded edge of the binding to the back of the quilt. Hand stitch the mitered corner edges and the first angled fold as well.

Sleeves and Documentation

Always make and attach a sleeve to the back of any quilt you make. This will keep future generations from nailing your quilt to the wall. When a sleeve is attached to a quilt, it is more likely to be hung properly.

Make the Sleeve

1. Cut a strip 8½″ × the actual finished width of your quilted quilt. Hem the short ends of the strip by turning under ¼″ toward the wrong side at each end of the strip. Press. Turn under another ¼″ at each end of the strip. Press. Topstitch the hems with matching thread.

2. Fold the strip in half lengthwise, wrong sides together. Match the raw edges and sew the sleeve strip into a tube.

3. Place the sleeve on your ironing board so that the seam is centered. Press the seam allowances open and press the sleeve flat.

4. Turn the sleeve over so the seam faces down. Press another crease along the length of the sleeve ½″ away from the fold at the top of the sleeve.

Second fold

First fold

5. Place the sleeve on the back of your quilt so that the seam allowance is hidden between the sleeve and quilt back. With the sleeve flat, be sure that the top fold is just below the top edge of the binding. Bring that fold down to expose the crease that is ½" away from it. This will give the sleeve fullness for the hanging rod. Pin the sleeve in place along this crease and the bottom edge of the sleeve.

6. Hand sew the sleeve to the back of the quilt, being careful that none of your stitches show through on the front.

Document Your Quilt

Make a documentation patch or label and sew it to the back of the quilt. Include information that you want people to know about your quilt. Your name and address, the date, the fiber content of the quilt, the pattern you used—this is important information. If you made the quilt for a special person or occasion, be sure to include that information as well.

Your documentation patch can be computer generated, embroidered, or handwritten with a fabric pen. Add appliqué, photo transfers—whatever seems right to you. *Be sure to document every quilt you make!* Your quilts are your legacy.

If you are going to print your documentation patch on an inkjet printer, consider using prepared fabric sheets from the Electric Quilt Company—we think they are the best on the market.

Hidden Documentation

We suggest writing or embroidering your name and the date directly on the quilt back, under the sleeve. Do this before you sew down the sleeve. If the documentation patch is ever removed, your name will remain on the quilt.

1. Make a label for your quilt.

2. Hem the edges of the label.

3. Hand stitch the label to the back of your quilt.

Signing Your Quilt

Painters sign the front of their paintings—quilters can sign the front of their quilts. We often sign our quilts in addition to putting a label on the back. There are a variety of ways to do this.

- Appliqué your name or initials and the date on the quilt top.

- Add information with embroidery or a permanent pen.

- Quilt your name and the date into your quilt with contrasting thread.

Projects

Nine different blocks and two border designs are in this book. We have used these blocks in a variety of ways, and we have even more ideas for ways to use them:

- Each block can be a small quilt to stand alone or to hang together with other blocks. You can make as many or as few of these quilts as you like.

- In some projects one block is repeated (pages 87, 90, and 93). The repetition of one design can be an engaging and powerful design element.

- Different blocks are combined with the borders to make a whimsical quilt that brings a smile to your face.

- Enlarge any block by 200% or more. Big, bold appliqué designs are attention grabbers. Add a border or borders and you'll have a stunner!

- Reduce the blocks to make miniature quilts. Use the cutaway appliqué technique (page 52) on very small pieces.

- Mix these appliqué blocks with pieced blocks. Remember that you can enlarge or reduce these patterns so that they fit the quilt you are making.

- Use the border patterns to make a panel quilt. Repeat one or both, add vertical sashing strips between them (or not), add borders … it'll be way cute!

- Make a house quilt by repeating the Going Home block (pullout page P2). Personalize the houses with embellisments.

- Make pillows for your sofa, chairs, or bed.

- Add some appliqué to your favorite tote bags.

- Repeat one block or combine blocks to make a long, narrow foot warmer quilt for the bottom of a bed.

There are hundreds of other ways you can use these blocks. We hope you find these ideas helpful. We know that you can take these ideas and the techniques you have learned and come up with many beautiful quilts!

Happy stitching!

All Together Now

Made by Linda Jenkins

Each finished quilt: 16½″ × 16½″

These cute quilts are designed to help you perfect your appliqué skills. You will enjoy making—and finishing—each one. Make them all and hang them together, as Linda has, or combine them in different groupings. Have fun mixing and matching them!

MATERIALS

The materials listed below are for one quilt. Repeat these materials for each small quilt.

> ### Fabric Note
> Linda used Moda Bella Solids for most of the backgrounds.

Block background: 1 fat quarter

Border: ⅛ yard

Appliqué: A variety of large scraps with the following exceptions:

The reverse appliquéd flower in the Passionate Flower block requires a square 16″ × 16″.

The large flower petals in the Big Flower block require ¼ yard.

Binding: ½ yard per quilt *or* 1¼ yards total for 9 quilts

Backing and sleeve: ⅝ yard per quilt *or* 5½ yards total for 9 quilts

Batting: 19″ × 19″ per quilt

Additional Supplies

Black Sharpie Ultra Fine Point Marker

Self-laminating sheets for templates (clear, single sided, heavyweight, 9″ × 12″): 1–2 sheets per block

Use *either* of the following products—you do not need both:

Clear or frosted upholstery vinyl (54″ wide): ½ yard for 1–3 blocks *or* 1⅓ yards for all 9 blocks for positioning overlays

OR

Quilter's Vinyl (16″ wide): ½ yard for 1 block *or* 3⅝ yards for all 9 blocks for positioning overlays

CUTTING

Block background:

Cut 1 square 16″ × 16″.

Borders:

Cut 2 strips 1¾″ × 14½″ for the side borders.

Cut 2 strips 1¾″ × 17″ for the top and bottom borders.

Cut fabric for appliqué as needed.

Binding:

Cut 1 square 17″ × 17″ to make a 2¼″-wide continuous bias strip at least 76″ long for each quilt. See Bias from a Square (page 72).
OR
Cut 1 square 43″ × 43″ to make a 2¼″-wide continuous bias strip 685″ long for all of the quilts. See Bias from a Square (page 72).

General Instructions

Refer to individual instructions for each quilt (pages 82–83) as needed and to appliqué patterns on pullout pages P1–P4.

1. Make templates and overlays for the blocks.

2. Press the backgrounds in half horizontally and vertically. Place the backgrounds on your design wall.

3. Cut out the appliqué pieces with their turn-under allowances. Place the appliqué pieces on the background on your design wall. Use the overlay to get them in the proper position or place them by eye. Play with your color and fabric choices until you are happy with the way your quilt looks.

> ### When Appliqué Extends Beyond the Block
> You will notice that some blocks have a bit of appliqué that extends beyond the edge of the block. If you are making individual 14″ × 14″ quilts, those bits of appliqué can be stitched over the borders or be cut off at the edge of the block. If you are combining blocks, you have the choice of appliquéing those bits over the sashing or borders.

4. Ideally you would audition all of the blocks together on the wall before you begin stitching. That is the best way to ensure that they will look great when they hang together. However, because this book is designed to help you learn many different appliqué techniques, you may find that you prefer to make one quilt at a time as you learn new techniques. If so, hang any blocks in progress along with any finished blocks on your design wall as you color new blocks.

5. Appliqué the blocks. Refer to the techniques for each block (starting on page 82).

6. When the appliqué is complete, press each block on the wrong side and trim it to 14½″ × 14½″.

Quilt Assembly

Seam allowances are ¼″.

1. Sew the side borders to the quilt. Press the seam allowances to the border.

2. Sew the top and bottom borders to the quilt. Press the seam allowances to the border.

3. Layer and baste the quilt (page 75).

4. Quilt by hand or machine.

5. Finish the quilt (page 77).

Instructions for Each Quilt

Leaves
Photocopy this pattern 1 time for templates.

TECHNIQUES USED

- Two-Part Leaves (page 63)
- Outer Points (page 42)
- Cutaway Appliqué (page 52) on the stems

Cotton Flowers
Photocopy this pattern 2 times for templates.

TECHNIQUES USED

- Outer Curves (page 58) and Circles (page 59)
- Outer Points (page 42)
- Cutaway Appliqué (page 52) on the stems
- Reverse Appliqué a Flower Center (page 67)

Lollipops
Notice that the stem lies over multiple circles in the two left flowers. In this case, the bottom three circles can be sewn together off-the-block. In the bigger flower on the right, the top three circles can be sewn off-the-block.

Photocopy this pattern 4–5 times for templates.

TECHNIQUES USED

- Outer Curves (page 58) and Circles (page 59)
- Outer Points (page 42)
- Cutaway Appliqué (page 52) on the stems
- Off-the-Block Construction (page 61) on the flowers

Wreath
This block is symmetrical, so you will trace the half-block provided on pullout page P3 onto your positioning overlay, and then rotate it 180° to trace the other half.

Note that the flower centers are all the same even though they are numbered differently. You can choose to sew one big scalloped flower or you can sew five different petals. The numbering sequence changes depending on which flower type you choose.

Which flower should you choose? It depends on the look you want and how hard you want to work. Inner points are slower and a bit more difficult to sew. But if you have chosen a fabric that looks better as one big piece, the single petal may be your best choice.

If you want to use different fabrics for the flowers, the five separate petals

may be the better choice. Although there are more petals, they are going to be faster to sew.

Wreath flower with single petal   Wreath flower with five petals

Photocopy this pattern 2–3 times for templates.

TECHNIQUES USED

- Outer Curves (page 58) and Circles (page 59)
- Outer Points (page 42) and Inner Points (page 49)
- Cutaway Appliqué (page 52) on the stems
- Off-the-Block Construction (page 61) on the flowers

Passionate Flower
This block has areas that can be reverse appliquéd: Linda reverse appliquéd the small petals in this block; Becky reverse appliquéd the larger flower in her quilt *The Garden at My House* (page 84). However, you can appliqué all of the shapes in the regular way, on top of the background. The choice is yours.

Note: To reverse appliqué the petals, begin by tracing the large flower onto the fabric you have chosen for it. Leave plenty of extra fabric around it. Use the positioning overlay to place the petal templates so that you can trace around them. Finger-press the edges of all the petals. Cut a square of fabric for the petals and pin or baste it in place under the flower fabric.

Reverse appliqué each petal and then appliqué the flower center. Press the flower. Turn it over and trim away the excess petal fabric, leaving a ³⁄₁₆″ seam allowance. The flower unit is now ready to finger-press and sew to the block.

Photocopy this pattern 2 times for templates.

TECHNIQUES USED

- Outer Curves (page 58) and Circles (page 59)

- Outer Points (page 42) and Inner Points (page 49)

- Reverse Appliqué a Flower Center (page 67)

If you sew this flower as a regular appliqué piece, trace around the large flower template onto the flower fabric. Finger-press the edges and pin or baste it on top of the background. We recommend using the Cutaway Appliqué technique (page 52).

Flower and Bird

Photocopy this pattern 2 times for templates.

TECHNIQUES USED

- Outer Points (page 42)

- Outer Curves (page 58) and Circles (page 59)

- Cutaway Appliqué (page 52) on the stem, bird legs, and beak

You can appliqué the eyes as normal on top of the bird. Or you can Reverse Appliqué (page 65) the bird's eyes or paint them on. The dark iris in each eye can be appliquéd, painted with a black paint pen, or sewn on using a button, bead, or other dark embellishment.

Going Home

The door #25 and door trim #26 are stitched together off-the-block. Since you cut through #26 to reveal the #25 fabric, this could be considered reverse appliqué. Or you can think of it as cutaway appliqué. No matter what, the two shapes are sewn together off-the-block.

Photocopy this pattern 2–3 times for templates.

TECHNIQUES USED

- Outer Points (page 42) and Inner Points (page 49)

- Outer Curves (page 58) and Circles (page 59)

- Cutaway Appliqué (page 52) on the #25/26 door, which is stitched using Off-the-Block Construction (page 61) along with #27

- Reverse Appliqué (page 65) on the windows and door #15

Vase of Flowers

Photocopy this pattern 3 times for templates.

TECHNIQUES USED

- Outer Points (page 42) and Inner Points (page 49)

- Outer Curves (page 58) and Circles (page 59)

- Cutaway Appliqué (page 52) on the stems and the flower shapes #24–#30

Big Flower

You can sew this block "with attitude" or with the invisible stitch.

This block is symmetrical, so you will trace the half-block provided on pullout page P3 onto your positioning overlay, and then rotate it 180° to trace the other half. Photocopy the half-block twice to make enough template pieces. Tape the center circle together, and then cover with laminate.

TECHNIQUES USED

- Outer Curves (page 58) and Circles (page 59)

- Appliqué with Attitude (page 69)

The Garden at My House

Top by Becky Goldsmith; machine quilted by Linda Jenkins

Finished quilt: 44½″ × 44½″

Don't you wish you could cover your house with pretty
fabric? Now you can! Sew a house to suit yourself
and let a marvelous garden grow around it.

MATERIALS

Block backgrounds: 1 fat quarter per block *or* 1 yard total

Sashing: ½ yard

Border: A variety to total 1⅓ yards

Appliqué: A variety of large scraps

Binding: ¾ yard

Backing and sleeve: 3¼ yards

Batting: 55″ × 55″

Additional Supplies

Self-laminating sheets for templates (clear, single sided, heavyweight, 9″ × 12″): 16 sheets

Black Sharpie Ultra Fine Point Marker

Use *either* of the following products—
you do not need both:

**Clear or frosted upholstery vinyl
(54″ wide):** 1¼ yards for positioning overlays

OR

Quilter's Vinyl (16″ wide): 3 yards for positioning overlays

CUTTING

Block backgrounds:

Cut 4 squares 16″ × 16″.

Border backgrounds:

Construct or cut from the lengthwise grain
2 strips 8″ × 35″ for the side borders.

Construct or cut from the lengthwise grain 2 strips
8″ × 47″ for the top and bottom borders.

Sashing:

Cut 6 strips 2″ × 40″. Subcut into

    A: 2 strips 2″ × 14½″

    B: 3 strips 2″ × 30″

    C: 2 strips 2″ × 33″

Cut fabric for appliqué as needed.

Binding:

Cut 1 square 26″ × 26″ to make a 2½″-wide
continuous bias strip 200″ long for the quilt.
See Bias from a Square (page 72).

Block Assembly

Refer to General Instructions (page 15) as needed and to the appliqué patterns on pullout pages P1–P4.

1. Make templates and overlays for the blocks.

2. Press the backgrounds in half horizontally and vertically. Place them on your design wall.

3. Cut out the appliqué pieces with their turn-under allowances. Place the appliqué pieces on the backgrounds on your design wall. Use the overlays to place the appliqué pieces in the proper position or place them by eye. Play with your color and fabric choices until you are happy with the way the blocks look.

> ### Audition the Entire Quilt
> Read ahead in these instructions. It's a good idea to get all of your sashing strips and borders (with the border appliqué pieces) on your design wall before you begin any stitching.

4. Appliqué the blocks. Refer to the suggested techniques as needed (pages 82–83).

Do not stitch any appliqué areas that extend beyond the edge of a block. These areas will be sewn down after the blocks are trimmed and sashed.

5. When your appliqué is complete, press the blocks on the wrong side and trim them to 14½″ × 14½″. Be careful not to trim away any appliqué that will be finished after sashing.

Border Assembly

1. Make templates and overlays for the borders, matching the appropriate borders along the join lines before tracing.

2. Piece your border backgrounds in a random pattern as Becky did or cut them from one fabric. Press the backgrounds in half horizontally and vertically. Place them on your design wall around the blocks.

3. Cut out the appliqué pieces with their turn-under allowances. Place the appliqué pieces on the border backgrounds on your design wall. Use the overlays to get the appliqué pieces in the proper position or place them by eye. Play with your color and fabric choices until you are happy with the way the borders look around your blocks.

4. Appliqué the borders, referring to the techniques below.

Floral Side Border

TECHNIQUES USED

- Outer Points (page 42)

- Outer Curves (page 58) and Circles (page 59)

- Bias Stems (page 73)

Floral Top and Bottom Border

TECHNIQUES USED

- Outer Points (page 42)

- Outer Curves (page 58) and Circles (page 59)

- Bias Stems (page 73)

5. When your appliqué is complete, press the borders on the wrong side. Trim the side borders to 6½″ × 33″. Trim the top and bottom borders to 6½″ × 45″.

Quilt Assembly

Refer to the quilt assembly diagram at right for quilt construction. Seam allowances are ¼″.

1. Sew the blocks together into rows with a sashing strip A between them. Press the seam allowances toward the sashing.

2. Sew the 2 rows of blocks together with a sashing strip B between them. Sew a sashing strip B to the top and the bottom of the quilt. Press the seam allowances toward the sashing.

3. Sew a sashing strip C to each side of the quilt. Press the seam allowances toward the sashing.

4. Sew the side borders to the quilt. Press the seam allowances toward the borders.

5. Sew the top and bottom borders to the quilt. Press the seam allowances toward the borders.

6. Layer and baste the quilt. Quilt by hand or machine.

7. Finish the quilt (page 75).

Quilt assembly diagram

Blowin' in the Wind

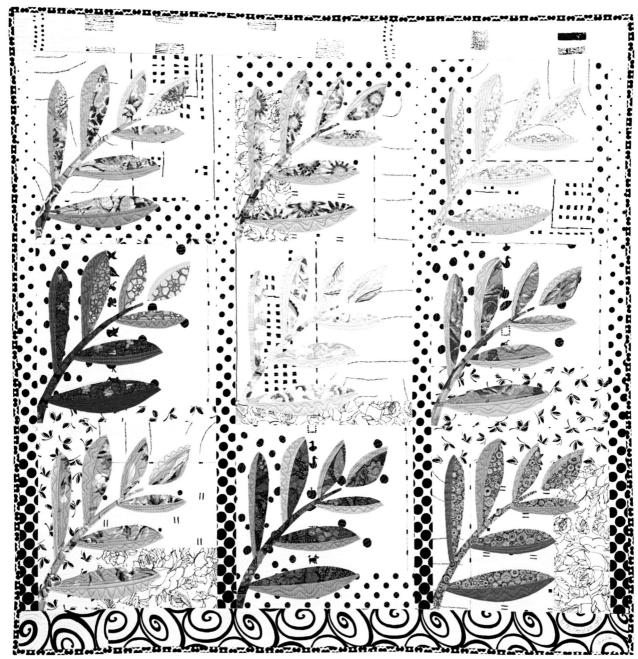

Made by Becky Goldsmith

Finished quilt: 48″ × 48″

Colorful leaves are waving in a breeze.
You can almost smell fresh tropical air!

MATERIALS

Fabric Note

Becky used a variety of black-and-white prints for all of her backgrounds. The most unusual fabric was designed by Yoshiko Jinzenji for Yuwa. She only had a yard of it, so she decided to combine it with other black-and-white fabrics.

These fabrics are sewn together in simple, random patterns to make each background square. You can do the same or cut your background squares from one or more fabrics.

Block backgrounds: 1 fat quarter per block *or* 2⅓ yards total

Vertical sashing: ⅓ yard (requires fabric at least 43″ wide, or additional fabric to piece strips)

Borders
Top border: ¼ yard

Bottom border: ¼ yard

or, if you use the same fabric for both the top and bottom borders: ⅓ yard

Appliqué: A variety of large scraps

Binding: ⅞ yard

Backing and sleeve: 3⅜ yards

Batting: 58″ × 58″

Additional Supplies

Black Sharpie Ultra Fine Point Marker

Self-laminating sheets for templates (clear, single sided, heavyweight, 9″ × 12″): 2 sheets

Use *either* of the following products—you do not need both:

Clear or frosted upholstery vinyl (54″ wide): ½ yard for positioning overlays

OR

Quilter's Vinyl (16″ wide): ½ yard for positioning overlays

CUTTING

WOF = width of fabric

Block backgrounds:
Cut or construct 9 squares 16″ × 16″.

Vertical sashing:
Cut or construct 4 strips 2″ × 42½″.

Top border:
Cut 2 strips 3½″ × WOF for the top border.

Bottom border:
Cut 2 strips 3½″ × WOF for the bottom border.

* If you use the same fabric for the top and bottom border, cut 3 strips 3½″ × WOF.

Cut fabric for appliqué as needed.

Binding:
Cut 1 square 27″ × 27″ to make a 2½″-wide continuous bias strip 215″ long for the quilt. See Bias from a Square (page 72).

Block Assembly

Refer to General Instructions (page 15) as needed and to the appliqué pattern on pullout page P1.

1. Make the templates and overlay for the block.

2. Place the backgrounds on your design wall and play with their placement until you are happy with the way they look together.

3. Press the backgrounds in half horizontally and vertically. Place them on your design wall.

Auditioning the Leaves

Refer to Two-Part Leaves (page 63), and notice that these leaves are easier to sew when the fabric on the bottom is cut bigger. However, it is difficult to see what the block will look like if you have big pieces of fabric on the wall during the audition. This is one of those times when it is best to cut all the pieces as you normally would, with a ³⁄₁₆″ turn-under allowance. After you know that the leaf fabrics you have chosen are the ones that work, you will need to recut the bottom fabric as directed on page 63.

4. Cut out the appliqué pieces with their seam allowances. Place the appliqué pieces on the backgrounds on your design wall. Use the positioning overlay to place the appliqué pieces or place them by eye. Play with your color and fabric choices until you are happy with the way the blocks look. Construct the leaves (page 63).

5. Appliqué the blocks as described on page 82.

6. When your appliqué is complete, press the blocks on the wrong side and trim them to 14½" × 14½".

Quilt Assembly

Refer to the quilt assembly diagram below for quilt construction. Seam allowances are ¼".

1. Sew the blocks together into columns. Press the seam allowances toward the bottom of the quilt.

2. Sew the 3 columns of blocks together with a vertical sashing strip between them. Press the seam allowances toward the sashing.

3. Sew a vertical sashing strip to each side of the quilt. Press the seam allowances toward the sashing.

4. Cut the selvages off the ends of the 2 top border strips. Sew the top border strips together, end-to-end. Press seam allowances to one side. Trim the top border to 3½" × 48½".

If your top and bottom borders are sewn from the same fabric, trim selvages off all 3 width-of-fabric strips. Sew the strips together, end-to-end, into 1 continuous strip. Trim to make 2 borders 3½" × 48½".

5. Cut the selvages off the ends of the 2 bottom border strips. Sew the bottom border strips together, end-to-end. Press seam allowances to one side. Trim the bottom border to 3½" × 48½".

6. Sew the top and bottom borders to the quilt. Press the seam allowances toward the borders.

7. Layer and baste the quilt. Quilt by hand or machine.

8. Finish the quilt (page 75).

Quilt assembly diagram

Fanciful Flowers

Made by Linda Jenkins

Finished quilt: 40″ × 40″

You've got to love the way these rings of flowers
seem to dance on this quilt!

MATERIALS

Light fabric: 1⅛ yards for backgrounds and sashing

Dark fabrics: A variety to total ⅞ yard for sashing and borders

Appliqué: A variety of large scraps

Binding: ¾ yard

Backing and sleeve: 3⅛ yards

Batting: 50″ × 50″

Additional Supplies

Black Sharpie Ultra Fine Point Marker

Self-laminating sheet (clear, single sided, heavyweight, 9″ × 12″): 1 sheet for templates

Use *either* of the following products—you do not need both:

Clear or frosted upholstery vinyl (54″ wide): ½ yard for positioning overlays

OR

Quilter's Vinyl (16″ wide): ½ yard for positioning overlays

CUTTING

WOF = width of fabric

Light fabric
Block backgrounds:
Cut 4 squares 16″ × 16″.

Sashing:
Cut 5 strips 1½″ × WOF. Cut each strip into 2 strips 1½″ × 20″ (10 total).

Cut 3 strips 4½″ × WOF. Cut these strips to make 18 squares 4½″ × 4½″.

Dark fabrics
Sashing:
Cut 5 strips 1½″ × WOF. Cut each strip into 2 strips 1½″ × 20″ (10 total),

or for more variety, cut 10 different strips 1½″ × 20″.

Borders:
Cut 3 strips 4½″ × 40″. Cut these strips to make 18 squares 4½″ × 4½″.

Cut fabric for appliqué as needed.

Binding:
Cut 1 square 25″ × 25″ to make a 2½″-wide continuous bias strip 180″ long for the quilt. See Bias from a Square (page 72).

Block Assembly

Refer to General Instructions (page 15) as needed and to the appliqué pattern on pullout page P3.

1. Make the templates and overlay for the block.

2. Press the backgrounds in half horizontally and vertically. Place them on your design wall.

3. Cut out the appliqué pieces with their turn-under allowances. Place the appliqué pieces on the backgrounds on your design wall. Use the overlay to get the appliqué pieces in the proper position or place them by eye. Play with your color and fabric choices until you are happy with the way the blocks look.

Refer to Off-the-Block Construction (page 61) and notice how the flower centers are sewn. Cut the flower center with its turn-under allowance for the audition. Recut it for sewing.

Audition the Entire Quilt

Read ahead in these instructions. It's a good idea to get all of your sashing strips and borders on your design wall before you begin any stitching.

4. Appliqué the blocks as described on page 82.

5. When your appliqué is complete, press the blocks on the wrong side. Trim them to 14½″ × 14½″.

Sashing Assembly

Seam allowances are ¼″.

1. Sew a light sashing strip to a dark sashing strip. Press to the dark strip. Repeat for all sashing strips.

2. Cut the pieced strips into pairs 1½″ × 2½″.

3. Construct 8 sashing strips A by sewing **7 pairs** together. Be sure to alternate light and dark fabrics. Press toward the dark fabric.

4. Construct 8 sashing strips B by sewing **8 pairs** together. Be sure to alternate light and dark fabrics. Press toward the dark fabric.

5. Place the sashing strips on your design wall around the blocks. Follow the quilt assembly diagram below to be sure that the sashing strips are turned the correct way. The light and dark squares are designed to alternate.

Border Assembly

Seam allowances are ¼".

1. Refer to the photo on page 90 and arrange the light and dark border squares on your design wall.

2. Sew light and dark squares together into pairs in each of the 4 borders. Press seam allowances toward the dark squares.

3. Construct 2 side border strips by sewing 4 pairs together for each border. Be sure to alternate light and dark fabrics. Press seam allowances toward the dark fabric.

4. Construct the top and bottom border strips by sewing 5 pairs together for each border. Be sure to alternate light and dark fabrics. Press seam allowances toward the dark fabric.

5. Place the border strips on your design wall around the quilt. Follow the quilt assembly diagram to be sure that the border strips are turned the correct way. The light and dark squares are designed to alternate.

Quilt Assembly

Refer to the quilt assembly diagram at right for quilt construction. Seam allowances are ¼".

1. Sew a sashing strip A to the sides of each block. Be careful to turn the sashing strips the correct way. Press seam allowances toward the block.

2. Sew a sashing strip B to the top and the bottom of each block. Be careful to turn the sashing strips the correct way. Press seam allowances toward the block.

3. Sew the blocks together into rows. Press the seam allowances in alternating directions.

4. Sew the rows together. Press the seam allowances toward the bottom of the quilt.

> ### Check the Direction of the Seam Allowances
> Sometimes seam allowances in a border strip will need to be pressed in the other direction so that they mesh with the sashing seam allowances. Check for this before you pin the border strips to the quilt. Re-press if needed.

5. Sew the side borders to the quilt. Be careful to turn the border strips the correct way. Press the seam allowances toward the borders.

6. Sew the top and bottom borders to the quilt. Be careful to turn the border strips the correct way. Press the seam allowances toward the borders.

7. Layer and baste the quilt. Quilt by hand or machine.

8. Finish the quilt (page 75).

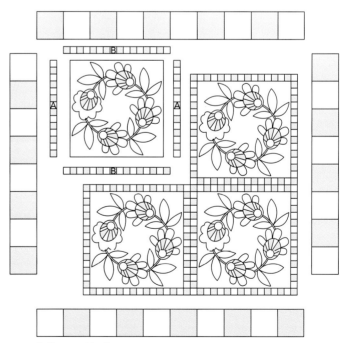

Quilt assembly diagram

Made by Becky Goldsmith

— Pretty Perky —

Finished quilt: 14″ × 56″

Doesn't this tall, skinny quilt remind you of red-and-white peppermint candies? It is wonderful to use on a narrow wall or as a table runner.

MATERIALS

Block backgrounds: 1 yard

Appliqué:

4 different fat quarters for the large petals in each block

A variety of large scraps for the remaining appliqué pieces

Binding: ¾ yard

Backing and sleeve: 2 yards

Batting: 24″ × 66″

Additional Supplies

Black Sharpie Ultra Fine Point Marker

Self-laminating sheets (clear, single sided, heavyweight, 9″ × 12″): 1 sheet for templates

Use *either* of the following products— you do not need both:

Clear or frosted upholstery vinyl (54″ wide): ½ yard for positioning overlay

OR

Quilter's Vinyl (16″ wide): ½ yard for positioning overlays

CUTTING

Block backgrounds:

Cut 4 squares 16″ × 16″.

Cut fabric for appliqué as needed.

Binding:

Cut 1 square 24″ × 24″ to make a 2½″-wide continuous bias strip 160″ long for the quilt. See Bias from a Square (page 72).

Block Assembly

Refer to General Instructions (page 15) as needed and to the appliqué pattern on pullout page P3.

1. Make the templates and overlay for the block.

2. Press the backgrounds in half horizontally and vertically. Place them on your design wall.

> ### Audition the Entire Quilt
> Read ahead in these instructions. It's a good idea to see all the blocks together on the wall before you begin to stitch.

3. Cut out the appliqué pieces with their turn-under allowances. Place the appliqué pieces on the backgrounds on your design wall. Use the overlay to get the appliqué pieces in the proper position or place them by eye. Play with your color and fabric choices until you are happy with the way the blocks look.

4. Appliqué the blocks as described on page 83. Becky used appliqué with attitude stitches (page 69) for all the appliqué in this quilt.

5. When your appliqué is complete, press the blocks on the wrong side and trim them to 14½″ × 14½″.

Quilt Assembly

Seam allowances are ¼″.

1. Sew the blocks together into a row. Press the seam allowances toward one end of the quilt.

2. Layer and baste the quilt. Quilt by hand or machine.

3. Finish the quilt (page 75).

About the Authors

Photo by Chad Mahlum Photography

The Green Country Quilter's Guild in Tulsa, Oklahoma, can be credited for bringing Linda Jenkins and Becky Goldsmith together. Their friendship developed while they worked together on many guild projects and through a shared love for appliqué. This partnership led to the birth of Piece O' Cake Designs in 1994 and has survived Linda's moves to Pagosa Springs, Colorado; back to Tulsa in 2001; and then to Grand Junction, Colorado, in 2008. Becky headed for Sherman, Texas, in 1994 and has stayed put since then.

Linda owned and managed a beauty salon before she started quilting. Over the years she developed a fine eye for color as a hair colorist and makeup artist. Becky's degree in interior design and many art classes provided a perfect background for quilting. Linda and Becky have shown many quilts and have won numerous awards. Together they make a dynamic quilting duo and love to teach other quilters the joys of appliqué.

In the fall of 2002 Becky and Linda joined the C&T Publishing family, where they happily remain.

For all of the notions mentioned in this book, how-to technique videos, and more:

Piece O' Cake Designs   www.pieceocake.com

Also by Becky Goldsmith and Linda Jenkins:

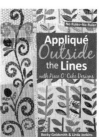

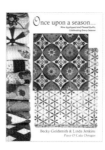
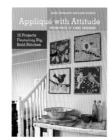

Great Titles and Products
from C&T PUBLISHING

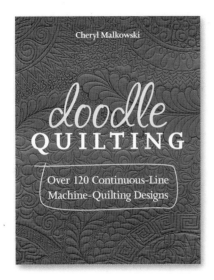

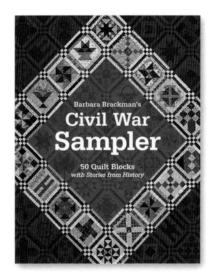

Available at your local retailer or **www.ctpub.com** *or* **800-284-1114**

For a list of other fine books from C&T Publishing, visit our website
to view our catalog online.

C&T PUBLISHING, INC.
P.O. Box 1456
Lafayette, CA 94549
800-284-1114

Email: ctinfo@ctpub.com
Website: www.ctpub.com

C&T Publishing's professional photography services are now available to
the public. Visit us at www.ctmediaservices.com.

Tips and Techniques can be found at www.ctpub.com > Consumer
Resources > Quiltmaking Basics: Tips & Techniques for Quiltmaking & More

For quilting supplies:

COTTON PATCH
1025 Brown Ave.
Lafayette, CA 94549
Store: 925-284-1177
Mail order: 925-283-7883

Email: CottonPa@aol.com
Website: www.quiltusa.com

Note: Fabrics shown may not be currently available, as fabric
manufacturers keep most fabrics in print for only a short time.